The Lion Roars

LETTERS TO THE CHARISMATIC CHURCH

Richard Moy

SHARING OF MINISTRIES ABROAD

Everyone is terrified when a lion roars –
and ordinary people become prophets
when the LORD God speaks.

Amos 3:8 (Contemporary English Version)

CONTENTS

Foreword

I'm a committed charismatic,[1] a conviction charismatic, a charismatic since the womb.

I've spent quite a few years researching charismatics, pastoring charismatics, helping lead charismatics.

But this last year may have been the hardest year to be a charismatic in my lifetime.

The reality is I love this movement.

I get the desire to have a leader you can truly get behind, be inspired by, and attribute great spiritual breakthroughs to. I've known a few.

I get the desire to move in miracles and wonder-working power.

I get the desire to build, build, build.

I get the personal intimacy with Jesus.

I get the cathartic expressionism.

---

[1] [Note for overseas readers: In the UK 'Charismatic' is a term that applies widely to churches which have experienced Holy Spirit renewal within the Church of England and other historic denominations, not just to 'new' churches. You can be evangelical, liturgical and charismatic. Charismatic does not mean prosperity theology but an openness to the Holy Spirit's graces and power].

I get the joy of hearing the voice of God.

I get the fascination with sensing God put words in your mouth that inspire/help/change other people.

I get the sheer humbling that occurs when you know that that was more than just you.

Because there is something about the charismatic church that has enabled people to experience God in a tangible way since the 1950s/60s, that released a pent up desire for discipling nations in the 'mission possible' era of the 1980s, that enabled repressed emotions to be healed in the 1990s, that kept going when others were giving up on God/theology/church in the 2000s, that propagated church plants and the Alpha course experience, that revived flagging churches and souls.

There's something about never letting disappointment in God or leaders be the final word.

But…there's also something about a section of the church that was going to change the world in the 1960s and 1970s, expected global revival in the 1980s, enjoyed hyper-expressivism in 1990s, built empires in the 2000s, assimilated into culture in the 2010s and has had to live with the disappointment of delayed desire for decades.

There's something about a section of the church where narcissism flourishes.

So while I've spent quite a few years researching charismatics, pastoring charismatics, helping lead charismatics, there are some truths I need to hear if I am not to throw the baby out with the bathwater.

I am a committed charismatic, a conviction charismatic, a charismatic till the grave.

And this is partly a series of comments I need to write to me.

(I hope they may be of some use to you too).

Introduction

10 years ago, I was with around 70 charismatic church leaders singing God's praises at Ashburnham Retreat Centre in Southern England. We were on the leaders retreat for the 'HTB network', a group associated with Holy Trinity Brompton (HTB), the home of the Alpha Course.

The visiting Vineyard USA speaker had brought a ministry support person with him to give prophetic words to the gathering. I was new, unknown in the network and sitting at the back. But he singled me out and said God would "greatly use my mind for the network." My ears pricked up because I had just signed up to do a doctorate in Theology in Ministry at Durham University. I was hoping to use this to help leaders keep going for the long run.

The first stage of the degree gave me the opportunity to do some basic field work.

I sought out three pairs of well-known church planters from the HTB network and interviewed them. The first pair were pioneer planters in the early 1980s, another pair planted in the 1990/2000s, and finally a younger pair of contemporaries whose relatively new churches had exploded into 500+ people (which in UK church terms is massive). I was looking for what sustained them in ministry. But I chanced upon three questions which opened the door to my final thesis.

- How would you define success in church planting?
- To what extent has success galvanised your work?
- When (if) you have had to, how do you cope with failure?

Their answers ranged from the honest, to the cathartic, to the harrowing.

It got me thinking how much the movement I was enjoying being part of was fuelled by a need to succeed.

It also got me thinking where that need to succeed may have come from, where that need to succeed could be good and godly, and where that need might massively undermine leaders?

How could leaders keep going if they couldn't keep pace with the success narrative?

So I began the research phase of the degree using the HTB network as my window into Contemporary Charismatic Christianity, encouraged by the then network leader Ric Thorpe.

But this four-year phase took me seven years to complete.

It was a journey that made me examine my own ministry and intentions, and one I very nearly didn't complete. I was being challenged and shaped by what I was writing and researching, and I could see the same thing happening to many of my interviewees. In addition, my wife Nicola and I were invited into a leadership role in the New Wine movement, with responsibilities across about seven dioceses in the South-East and a chance to observe and sometimes contribute to national decision making, so we were getting another front seat to observe and participate in another part of the UK charismatic church that served a range of denominations, but was led almost exclusively by people with a very similar charismatic Anglican heritage to those I was studying in the HTB network.

With all this going on I found I had a need to pause. I was missing something in my research I couldn't quite put my finger on. It was a lonelier task now I was on the remote research phase, and God was working on me while I was writing, which was beginning to be an uncomfortable process.

I just needed a break.

This need proved to be the making of my research. Durham granted me a year out in 2017-2018 and around the same time I spoke to Sandy Millar who had some great advice. 'If you want to understand the history of Charismatic Renewal in the Church of England you need to speak to John Collins. He knows more about Renewal in the Anglican Church than anyone else living.'

Collins had been senior curate at All Souls Langham Place (1951-1957) when it exploded into life under John Stott. He had been at St Mark's Gillingham as vicar firstly seeing rapid church growth with David Watson and David MacInnes as his curates, and then after they had left, stewarding a mini revival in 1963, that left him persona non grata with Anglican Evangelicals and Bishops alike. He eventually moved to rural Dorset and saw another explosion of spiritual life at Canford parish. This led to the planting of the Lantern Church with John and Eli Mumford (later of Vineyard UK) who Collins also stewarded into Charismatic Christianity. Collins was then head hunted back to be vicar of HTB, led an exceptional team and had the rare sense to know when to get out of the way and hand on to Sandy Millar, becoming Millar's curate for his final years. Millar was one in a long list of outstanding Christian leaders that John Collins was only too happy to release. After finally leaving HTB in 1989 Collins continued to mentor people, especially ordinands. Right into his 90s he started each day with 90-minute devotions with a Greek New Testament and a commentary. He finally went to glory in late 2022.

So rather than continuing with my thesis, 2017-2018 year was punctuated by regular trips to see John Collins.

My first encounter with Collins had been two years previously when I had chauffeured some lifelong friends of his to meet him. Their deep love was wonderful to see. It was evident again that year as I met and interviewed Collins' former Canford and Gillingham teams at David and Clare MacInnes' house. It was evident when I spoke to his curates and key lay ministers from HTB. It was a love grounded in years of praying and reading the bible together in daily staff times and by shared experience and respect for one another. And there was a lot of laughter and fun.

John's perspective filled out the edges of my thinking and gave a far clearer picture of the people and issues I was researching, When I returned to write up my thesis his story and insights became a backbone to a thesis that explored HTB's roots in an evangelicalism Collins personified.

Having been immersed in the New Wine and HTB worlds I gained a further opportunity to observe the charismatic church in the UK and beyond.

In 2020 I was invited by a trustee to apply for an itinerant ministry role as National Director of SOMA UK.

SOMA is the New Testament Greek word for 'body' and stands for 'Sharing of Ministry Abroad'. It has a particular call to 'join the Holy Spirit tending to the nervous system of the body of Christ'. It came out of a 1978 pre-Lambeth conference gathering of international charismatic/renewed bishops and was championed by men like Michael Harper (another of John Stott's former curates) and Bishop David Pytches (who also founded New Wine).

As I researched SOMA I was struck by its source of power. Looking at its foundation documents more than half of their planning meetings was prayer together. It was a movement grounded in intercession. Small wonder that the Spirit broke out in the run up to that Lambeth Conference. Small wonder that Global Majority bishops found their voice a week later to steer Anglicanism at what could have been one of its rockiest points.

A year after being recruited I began as National Director. As Covid restrictions eased I started to travel and saw some of the fruit from renewal ministry over the decades.

Back in the UK although the early days of renewal cost people like John and Diana Collins 'preferment' (promotion) and possibility, by 2023 charismatic Christianity (renewal) has become an accepted norm. It involves little challenge to power as it is in power. Those in power use charismatic jargon to justify all kinds of developments. What is generally lacking is actual spiritual power.

We see that when we send our SOMA teams to learn and serve with our contacts around the world. For years teams have been going out saying they learnt more than they gave. Now we are going out almost in desperation, praying that we can bring back olive branches of hope to the church in the UK.

And we do.

The demons flee.

The sick are healed.

The teams are accelerated in their spiritual life.

And they bring back hope from a Global church that has grown up.

SOMA is necessary because the nervous system of the body of Christ has a purpose. It wakes up the sleeping parts of the body when there is pain elsewhere. We see that also through the work of all sorts of bigger charities like IJM and Open Doors. When people hear of the hurt in the world and persecution the global church faces only those they are too deeply comatose by creature comforts fail to stir a little, and many find themselves waking up.

So, this little book comes from these stories, from my work with New Wine, HTB, and SOMA, as well as from our local church, from my reading on Wesley, Whitefield, Wimber and Stott and revival, from running seminars and teaching and preaching around the country and nation.

As I write I am acutely aware that the past 12 months have been some of the worst and most horrific for charismatic Christianity in the UK I can remember.

This is not because of persecution or opposition from without.

In fact, we have been in a time of unprecedented favour within denominations and other groupings, with the central Church of England financing millions of pounds a year of culturally charismatic initiatives.

The tragedies of this year have been the exposing of some of our champions as being less than they ought to be.

This has been seen in the ecclesiastical powers that be bending their knee to hidden spiritual powers. It has been seen in moral failings around abuse. It has been seen in abuse of power by speakers we have platformed. It has been seen in a spirit of timidity, exhaustion or fear of failure that makes leaders into voluntarily caged birds when we need the generals to rise up. It has been a shocking year for the charismatic church.

Despite this 2023 was also a year with at least one clear indication of hope in the Western Church. A genuinely humble awakening seemed to happen for a season in the Spring among Gen-Z students in Ashbury, Kentucky. This has stirred many hearts and provoked several abortive attempts at simulation. But could it be that churches, intercessors and leaders who have become charismatic in name only now hear the call to holiness and prayer and help awaken us once again?

Chapter One:
Remember – The Baby In The Bathwater

Dear friends,

Remember the baby in the bathwater.

If you're ever thinking of giving up on the charismatic church, giving up on 'renewal', why not pause for a moment and remember how you came into it? Was it all in one go? Was it slow or sudden? Gentle or dramatic? Was it an immersion, a saturation, or a sprinkling? Was it perhaps something you have always known and not quite realised was there… a birth right, building on the legacy of those around you?

I came into the charismatic movement thrice: Once in the womb and early upbringing, once in Romania as a teenager and once, like many, through the Alpha Course Holy Spirit Away Day.

My Story:

My parents were converted in the 1970s into the North Fellowships as older teenagers. I've listened to tapes of the founder GW North teaching, and from what I can tell he was the real deal charismatic leader. He didn't want to market the gospel, so all his works were self-published. He had a clear healing ministry, and a love-filled heart, with mystical tendencies. It seems the North Fellowships were keen on young converts 'breeding for the Kingdom' and so I came into the charismatic movement in the womb, no doubt surrounded by three chord choruses, tongues and prayer meetings and perhaps even like Jeremiah with an emergent call. Some of my earliest months were spent being cared for in the pastor's house and I imagine I was well prayed for in this time.

As a child I remember singing to God quite naturally, devoutly joining in the prayers at my brother's dedication when I was 5 and moved by the water baptisms of our lodger and others in our little church. Later we moved into a large FIEC church, the Worthing Tabernacle, under Tony Sergeant's ministry. Tony was a wonderful man who had studied the importance of 'unction' (Holy Spirit anointing) in Dr Martyn Lloyd-Jones's preaching ministry. I was similarly moved at the 'Tab' by visits from Ishmael (charismatic singer/ writer) his dancing daughter, and missionaries like Jackie Pullinger who had seen addicts delivered in Hong Kong as she prayed in tongues and Richard Wurmbrand who had supernaturally survived communism in solitary confinement in Romania. On church camps and Scripture Union camps I committed my life to Jesus at every opportunity and remember a tangible experience of the Spirit on a Norfolk sailing boat.

But life in the UK is attritional on young believers and by the time I was 17 I needed to get a thousand miles away from my parents, church and school to have a full conversion. Even then it nearly didn't stick. In 1995, when the charismatic movement was in full swing in the UK, I went to a cessationist Baptist church for a week of outreach in a village in a remote corner of Romania. There I encountered a filling with the Spirit that overwhelmed me, left me repenting deeply and wanting to read Scripture, sing and (eventually) testify. And testify I did the night after conversion to 70+ villagers and campers. I found God answered my prayer of the previous night to 'give me the words'. Words have kept flowing ever since, and a nervous wannabe public speaker was turned into a boy/man who found to his enormous surprise that people listened when he spoke. I came back to England, got baptized, gave my testimony in a sixth-form assembly to my 16-18-year-old peers, got discipled by my teacher David Cook (using JI Packer's Knowing God and Mark's gospel) and my pastor Gordon Steer and his wife Ruth who hosted me each week so I could attend youth group. I read scores of missionary stories, was invited to preach, lead a youth camp and do all sorts of things – and still I nearly blew it.

The pastor from Romania who impacted me straight after the conversion was a godly man called Adi Popa. Astonishingly talented, I imagine he could have led almost any organization and he played music at concert levels. He had invested his life in church planting in communist and post-communist Romania. He had a crown of thorns over one of the doors in his humble home and lived with his family off fifty dollars a month and the proceeds of a family allotment. His evangelism technique was to translate Wimber/Vineyard songs, play them on his Casio keyboard in a market square, gather a crowd (often of hecklers/persecutors) and then preach the gospel to them. By my second visit in 1997 I think four churches had been started this way.

So when in 1996, nine months or so after my conversion, he came to the UK I felt like it was the second coming of Jesus. Although I'd read through the New Testament several times and the Old Testament in a few months (10 chapters a day), and had all this mentoring investment, I still strayed from a close walk with Jesus. And as I did so I took it out on his church…I pointed a finger saying, 'the church is rubbish, the church is hypocritical, if only the church was holy…' when all the while I guess I was pointing three fingers back at me. That weekend I had a grace encounter, a baptism in the Spirit encounter, and a harrowingly tough conviction encounter.

Grace, Baptism and Conviction Encounters

Meeting Adi Popa again was a pure grace encounter. Ashamed and afraid to see him, all I met was love, recognition and acceptance. So the next morning I knew I wanted more time with him. As he was keyboardist for the Alpha Course away day, I duly gate-crashed. Nicky Gumbel was on the VHS videos from the height of the Toronto Blessing explosion era of the Alpha Course explaining his encounters with the Spirit, praying in tongues and how to be filled again with the Spirit. We then started to sing a song Adi had translated into Romanian and we as a church sang regularly, *As The Deer*, but there were lines I just could not sing. I realised I had lost the joy of my salvation and lost everything that was most precious to me. I'd lost the treasure more costly than gold – I couldn't truly sing lyrics that stated 'God alone was my heart's desire'.

I took a hymn book and a bible to a balcony in the church, desperate to get back this treasure I had lost. I repented on my knees, cried out to God, and found that my words were flowing in a new language, not my own. Apparently when I finally came down the stairs my face was glowing. I felt like a brand-new man. Aged 17 I could do anything for the Lord. I would 'Attempt great things of God. Expect great things of

God,' as one of my favourite missionary authors read that year, Hudson Taylor, movingly said, and 'serve the purposes of God in my generation.'

But the Holy Spirit hadn't finished His work with a grace encounter, or a (re-) baptism encounter. He still had a conviction encounter with purifying fire to bring.

On Sunday I attended the morning and evening services as usual but was unexcited that the evening speaker was the cover speaker for the pastor. Yet God worked through that man Roger Chilman in the most remarkable way. As he had been preparing on Ezra, God had overwhelmed him and given him what seemed to him like a divine dictation based on Israel purifying themselves from the harrowing passages at the end of the book.

You would have to know Roger to realise how unusual an event this was, and he knew that himself.

So, he took it to Pastor Gordon, who weighed it, introduced it with an interview with Roger, and then had someone read the scripture text. From the moment the Bible was read I realised this was for me and, once more, I became overwhelmed with sorrow, conviction and repentance. I realised that God was telling me what I needed to give up now. The Scripture came alive, and I was backed into a corner by God and made to reckon with my sin again. I'm not sure I even heard most of Roger's divine dictation as I was already under full conviction and had run out to the kitchen. There the elderly organist consoled me that it doesn't get much easier even in old age.

After a long and heart-breaking encounter, I resolved to go God's way. The Spirit of Holiness won. The next day I stumbled through a difficult and costly conversation leaving behind one way of life and eventually pushing forward to another.

There were other re-entries into a Spirit-filled life, as I often needed top-ups. Early experiences included on 'Operational Mobilisation' Love Europe in Hungary where I was blown away by the freedom in worship of the smiley blond guy standing next to me. In Newfrontiers I encountered God powerfully each week and especially when I was at Stoneleigh Bible week. This was the era of enjoying the Toronto Blessing. A wonderful moment came at HTB in London a few months later when Sandy Millar prayed for me under the pulpit and gently helped me to embrace my new calling into the Church of England.

Your Story

What's your story? Maybe you're more like Ivor Saunders? Ivor was my fellow curate at St Jude's Wolverhampton in 2004. He didn't let the disappointment of not becoming a vicar in his 20s define him. Instead, he was ordained in his 60s to serve the church he had already ministered in since his teenage years. He modelled a steady walk with the Lord that grew year by year.

It's not about how dramatic it is. It's about the Spirit's work in you. You may have had wonderful experiences, dramatic journeys, deep repentances. You may have faithfully walked with God and not needed a spiritual showground rollercoaster to take you briefly to the heights.

Our Story

The charismatic story is often described as 'waves' of God's blessing.

First Wave: Pentecostalism

These waves are all the after-effects of the big (world changing) first wave which was the rise of Pentecostalism. It is really worth reading about William J Seymour and the 1906 Azuza Street revivals if you don't know the story.

As branches of Pentecostals developed, they would 'tarry' [which meant 'wait intently'] for a "Baptism of the Spirit" often 'travailing in fasting and prayer' for days until they got the experience. Branches of Pentecostalism exploded around the world as the experience of God's power, expectation of growth, tendency for new churches to split, and low structural bar to leadership meant that anyone with a passion could start their own church That is a great story in itself, but we pick up the story 50 years later in the UK when an overspill of Pentecostalism began to very obviously impact the mainline denominations through people like Dennis Bennett and Arthur Wallis.

Second Wave: Early Renewal

In the late 1950s and early 1960s charismatic pioneers from the USA and UK had given the churches in England a spiritual jumpstart – occasionally with a little too much voltage. By the time I was born in the late 1970s the 'second wave' of charismatic renewal ministry was nearly 20 years old. In the late 1970s there were a string of house fellowships around the country sometimes aligned into emergent groups who would ultimately operate a bit like denominations if they outlived their founders. Many of these were made up of people who used to be Baptist, Anglican or Brethren.

Some of the leaders, were restorationists in their theology. They believed that God was going to bypass the old denominations, restore his reign and rule and start again with a newer purer church. It was a time of real excitement in the churches, spiritual growth, renewal, conversions and a sense of rediscovering the New Testament church (both good and bad bits).

But there were others who had carved out a renewal space within denominations like the Church of England.

If it cost a lot for some leaders like Colin Urquhart to leave Anglicanism and start again, it cost even more for some others to stay. Michael Harper, David Watson and others broke some ground within a denomination, but it was a slow and potentially atrophying journey to attempt to change a denomination around. Harper eventually left. Watson died early. John Collins had to fight hard to justify being a charismatic.

Early charismatics of all flavours did hard graft bible study to justify their experiences to biblically literate counterparts. They searched the Scriptures, tested the spirits, learnt to have joy in discovery and sometimes lost their jobs, churches, and friends for it.

Collins was ostracised by his former champions and mentors, but through it all he grew strong. The renewal at the dockers' church of St Mark's Gillingham, became the renewal at the rural Dorset church of Canford, and as he took teams around the country he set fires blazing elsewhere, including at HTB some years before he was made vicar.

Reports of the state of renewal by 1980 are varied. There are indications renewal may have reached its zenith in the mid-1970s as barriers blurred with other forms of spiritual practice around it. But that is certainly not the whole story. My own organisation, SOMA UK (Sharing of Ministries Abroad) was born out of a charismatic gathering of Bishops at the 1978 Lambeth Conference and an inspirational amount of prayer that went into the planning of this gathering. Tom Smail was a significant writer and theologian. David Watson was still a prominent charismatic Anglican minister and David DuPlessis had recently prayed for a young barrister called Sandy Millar to be filled with the Spirit. Sandy Millar was already busy passing on David Watson's teaching on the Spirit to fellow ordinands at Cranmer Hall in the mid-1970s. From there he returned to Holy Trinity Brompton as curate of what was still an 'establishment church'. Holy Trinity was led by a conservative evangelical vicar Raymond Turvey who also open to see the church move in the power of the Spirit.

But there were definitely signs that Renewal was stagnating in the face of opposition. Being open to the Spirit was a cross to bear for Turvey and for many other vicars around the country who had been touched by renewal but found themselves up against immovable parish forces. As late as 1992 the church Nicola and I now serve in Chiswick, London, was almost shut by the Bishop of Kensington. Elements of the congregation of Christ Church Turnham Green couldn't cope with a more informal monthly family service and the outgoing vicar had said 'you are crucifying me' as he flung his keys back to his wardens in a heated vestry discussion. This sort of story was replicated across the country.

So, when in 1980 HTB was looking for a charismatic vicar to work with Sandy and his 'bright young things', Sandy truly believed that there were only 3 or 4 charismatic clergymen in England who could do the job. Sandy's bright young things included 'the 5 Nicky's and Ken', a group that included future vicar and churchwarden Nicky Gumbel and Ken Costa. They had come down to London after conversions in a Cambridge Mission led by David MacInnes, and this group would form a key part of the backbone of HTB for the next 45 years. Millar was delighted that MacInnes' former vicar John Collins was appointed to HTB, and even played a part in recruiting him.

Third Wave: Wimber:

It was Collins' HTB and with David Pytches' St Andrew's Chorleywood that would be the key places in England to receive John Wimber, styled himself as a 'fat man trying to find his way to heaven'. Wimber was an American former pop-musician who taught Power Healing and Church Planting, and how to grow churches through mid-sized communities where everyone gets to play.

If 1960s and 1970s renewal in England was often a refreshing stream trickling through the English countryside, the Wimber revolution (known as the 'Third Wave' following Pentecostalism and 1960s/70s Renewal), would be a mighty torrent, not always appreciated by some. The HTB network, Alpha Course as we know it, New Wine and Soul Survivor would almost certainly not have existed without his influence. Wimber made it fun and in doing so fundamentally altered liturgical, ecclesiastical and worship patterns in the UK.

Fourth Wave? Toronto Blessing

A final wave – **The Toronto Blessing** – which roughly spanned 1994-1998 has become the brackish bathwater we charismatics have been swimming in for the past 25 years. There has not been anything comparable since. It was a wave in part rejected by Wimber for excesses, but there was much good in it. Among the English it was particularly helpful for those needing emotional healing and the touch of the Father's love. Upper-middle-class English clergymen and lay people, often the products of a boarding school system or wartime parents, seemed to particularly benefit from it, as wounds from remote relationships with parents were healed by a tangible sense of the Father's love. It was an experience that coincided with the launch of the Alpha Course on a national/international stage and that experience remains enshrined in the Holy Spirit weekend/day away.

In some ways the experience of love at Toronto propelled churches into social action, in other ways it accelerated a 'me-centred' turn in the charismatic world. Where the price of entry in the early Wimber years had been 'I surrender all', the price of entry post-Toronto was 'I need love/therapy'. The Spirit was something I could call on whenever I needed a pick-me-up.

Loving the baby

But I want to finish with my own story from the late 1990s. I was attending a University Christian Union house party when I met a charismatic undergraduate for whom Sunday church was the highlight of his week as he loved the tangible presence of God so much. That summer I met a passionate worshiper in Hungary. As I moved into Newfrontiers (NFI) in 1998 I discovered that this life of worship, moving in gifts of the Spirit and honing abilities to hear from God were the real deal. I prayed, studied, repented, fasted, grew, failed, recommitted, stepped out and wanted to be a history maker, who knew that it was true today that 'when people prayed cloudless skies would break and Kings and Queens will shake'. I wanted to serve the purpose of God in my generation. I loved the Scriptures. I loved my raw, immature experiences of God. I loved being a charismatic and I knew that what we had – Toronto, Wimber, Renewal – whatever – had the ability to change the world. I was connected to the power that raised Jesus from the dead – my Father in heaven, working through His Spirit.

If the charismatic movement is a relative baby within church history, it is a precious baby indeed. And if at times it behaves like it is a baby/infant still it is surely a deeply loved child of God and one that is well worth nurturing.

Dear friends, let us not chuck out the baby with the bathwater.

Chapter Two:
Remember, The Bathwater Needs Flushing

Dear friends,

A while ago I had a prophetic picture at a gathering of SOMA International leaders where I saw a baby carefully wrapped in swaddling bands being handed to us. This was our inheritance as a charismatic renewal movement. A precious gift, a much younger sibling to Pentecostalism, and an infant compared to its great uncles, the Evangelical Revival and the Reformation, and a newborn in contrast to its far older ancestors with clear roots in the early church.

The charismatic movement that has been so lovingly handed on to our generations is a precious spiritual baby. But it is a baby that has been swimming in some pretty murky bathwater.

What are these murky waters?

Partly they are murky because they hide something.

Recently we have been reeling from delayed revelations. Whenever we talk about a 'culture of honour', we 'preach the positives' or we turn a blind eye to the failings of a megastar/movement because we crave their success, we run the gambit of delayed revelation. Delayed because we put it off. Revelation because everything hidden will one day be revealed. Gambit because delayed revelation reeks destruction.

I tend to get more knocked than my wife does when a scandal breaks out. I think it's because I think I am still somehow searching for a hero, a spiritual John Wayne (or John Wesley) I can join in with, whereas she has a more realistic assessment of people. I get equally disappointed in myself. She keeps a more even keel. But as destructive as these scandals can be, the answer is not to keep things in the dark, but to bring them to the light. While we hide in false optimism or rank denial it gets more and more obvious to those around us that our 'baby' isn't getting any cleaner. We've come to the point that the bathwater needs emptying, and if we're honest, the point when this 'baby' of renewal needs to grow up.

It is not always a culture of honour that causes us as trustee boards, staff, family, church members, and institutions to protect a wayward star or protect ourselves. Sometimes it is fear: 'If anyone knew this what would happen?' So it takes 25 years for a young worship leader's story to be believed. Sometimes it is blind faith: 'It couldn't be him/her, they're so close to God.' So no-one believes the reports of the masseuse claiming abuse, or the volunteers at the community serving disabled people. Sometimes it is loyalty: 'I/we owe everything to them.' So we keep our head down and hope it will get better. Sometimes it is a misplaced sense of common failings: 'We all have faults/who am I to judge?' So we send them away/onto the next role and allow abuse to be perpetuated in another part of God's world. Perhaps most tragically, sometimes it is simply finance: 'What would happen to our "goose that laid the golden eggs" if everyone knew the goose was really a pigeon?

But let justice flow like a river and wash out the bathtub again.

We have to be better at recognising our own failings as a movement.

If everything will one day be revealed it is because the Lord wants truth to be known.

In eternity we will be 'fully known even as we fully know' and we will be praising the Lamb in wonder, awe and admiration that he allowed any of us to enter His Father's home with him. There will be an apocalypse. An unveiling. And right now on this earth there seems to be an unveiling too. It is several years on from the #metoo movement, the Jimmy Saville scandal in the UK and the aftermath of George Floyd in the USA and we've just been through the murder of Nahel. M in Paris by police. It seems that this is an era in God's economy where formerly untouchable men (and some women) and institutions of power are being brought into the light and held accountable for their crimes, failings and wrongdoings.

But while there have been real and culpable faults and crimes in leaders, there have also been systemic, cultural flaws within movements and institutions that need addressing. These can be just as hard to spot and ultimately more damaging. They are often justified by a concern for the 'greater good', or 'God's Kingdom' but before long can easily take us in completely different path where the only kingdoms we are protecting are our own.

Systemic Faults – the Making of Many Hagars

Let's pause for a moment and consider the biblical story of our father in faith, Abram who became Abraham:

Abram was promised an inheritance to make a prosperity teacher blush. The stars in the sky, the sand of the seashore would pale in comparison with his descendants. But the promise was a long time coming. So when it was suggested that he father a child through a (presumably) younger and more virile woman than his wife, we read that he took the chance. Ishmael was born to his #babymama Hagar. Hagar was his shortcut to the promised glory.

Hagar, despite keeping her end of the bargain was then driven out into the desert when wife #1 finally had the child of promise. This was one of the many Old Testament #metoo moments. Sarah's son's name Isaac means he laughs, but there wasn't much laughter going on for #babymama Hagar when she was driven out. Instead, she was driven to the point of despair for not just her life but also the life of the 'Father of Faith's' eldest son.

It takes an angel from God to intervene, but not before we get an early megaphone clue in Scripture that even the poster boy 'man of faith', Abraham, and the chosen one Sarah, can hurt a lot of people on the way. The God of the Beatitudes is often found sitting with their castoffs outside the camp. Blessed are those who mourn. Blessed are the Hagars.

Back to today, and it doesn't take long to realise that there have been a lot of Hagars in the charismatic movement.

Hagars who have been used to serve a God-given vision and spat out when no longer able to act as a short-cut to institutional growth.

A lot of the bathwater around the charismatic movement has to do with the way that we have made 'Jesus' into a commodity for profit and for power.

This leads us to use and misuse people, use and misuse hope and aspirations, to use and misuse platforms, to use and misuse truth and Scripture, to use and misuse finances, and to use and misuse power.

How many Hagars have been hurt along the way because they are no longer convenient or economically viable to us? Discarded like a once famous Hollywood starlet? Quietly ignored like an unacknowledged aide? Unthanked and unnoticed until they drop out, burn out, level out or quietly leave? Then simply replaced when the next shiny person comes along? It brings a tear to my eye when I realise my part in that.

The Hagar syndrome is an apt analogy for how it can feel to work for a Christian organisation. If you give your body and soul for the cause and get sent away into the night with a non-disclosure (NDA) clause slapped on you then you're a Hagar. It can be even worse if you're also expected to endure a handshake/prayer/platitude as you get discarded into the night.

Yes, it happens.

Yes, it happens far too often.

How in heaven's name did we become business minded organisations who protect their 'spiritual legacy' at the expense of those who serve alongside us? May God have mercy on us all.

These are techniques we hold in common with any number of secular organisations, but we compound it with the illusion of shared purpose and shared family identity. So there is a 'one hand on the shoulder' prayer ministry and another hand holding a dagger in their back' as a former staff member is shoved out of the door. Imagine having to endure that from your persecutors/former employers. Imagine Abraham and Sarah praying for Hagar as she was sent into a wilderness desert. Ultimately in God's Kingdom all NDAs will be disclosed. Truth is truth. Wouldn't it be better to face the music now than have to face the face of Christ on that day and be held to account for all we have done?

Hagars abound.

Hagars will receive God's blessing – even if those carrying a fraction of Abraham and Sarah's anointing shove them out.

If we are honest sometimes the Hagars have to go because they remind us of failure, or because we have grossly overestimated our own spiritual success trajectory. Yes, there may be some others who needed a push out of the nest, some who just couldn't do their job, some who no longer believed what they signed up for. But this fear of fear of failure, and stifled success is chronic.

Charismatics have been notorious for overpromising and under delivering.

A new day is always dawning – but it's always just around the corner.

I've just heard of a flagship charismatic church that has had to lay off over half its staff team.

But this is not a new issue.

Rob Warner's analysis shows that charismatics overall experienced a 16% decline in the 1990s (and that was during a decade that was supposed to be the heyday of the Toronto blessing, the decade of evangelism and the rise of Alpha). Yet nevertheless 79% of those same charismatic churches were expecting a large growth in the early 2000s. Warner writes:

"Optimistic expectations have become heightened beyond reality as a result of embracing later-modern assumptions of assured growth and success. Moreover, this ideology appears to have become unfalsifiable: if success is the automatic and intrinsic destiny of the true church, whenever churches suffer decline, it can only be, according to the law of inherent and assured growth because they are not Evangelical, Pentecostal or Charismatic enough… there has been a zealous stroking of vision inflation… when their growth expectations wantonly disregard the fact that the decade of evangelism has been a decade of decline evangelicals in general and charismatics in particular appear to be in denial … and exemplify Festinger's account of the characteristic response to cognitive dissonance – a defiant optimism that is essentially an escapist fantasy to sustain implausible convictions."[1] (Rob Warner)

Selling a dream

We can misuse hopes and dreams as well as people. A peculiarly charismatic part of the murky bathwater is the selling of spiritual hope, aspirations and dreams. It is a cyclical dream of imminent instant success couched in revivalism. This dream keeps coming round, and is then sent out into the wilderness to die.

---

[1] Warner, R: Fissured Resurgence: Developments in English pan-evangelicalism, 1966-2001, 130, https://kclpure.kcl.ac.uk/portal/files/2929985/430439.pdfp.130 [accessed 19.3.2021].

One of our issues is we rarely hold up our hands where we have got it wrong. I remember being a young student in the mid-1990s, printing copies of the 2 Chronicles 7:14 promise, "if my people, who are called by my name will humble themselves and pray…" for other people to put up in their university bedrooms to match my one. I was dreaming non-stop of revival from my conversion onwards. In some ways it was because I wanted everyone to experience what I did. In other ways it was because I wanted this Christian thing to work – and work in a way I liked. O that all my college/school would bow the knee as I (thought I) had to Jesus. When my pastor's wife commented, 'wouldn't it be amazing to see revival in your school,' I retorted, hyper-confidently, 'wouldn't it me amazing to see revival in right across the South of England' (I'm not sure where my geographical boundary came from, but I had never lived as far north at London at that stage).

When my pastor's wife commented, 'wouldn't it be amazing to see revival in your school,' I retorted, hyper-confidently, 'wouldn't it be amazing to see revival in right across the South of England.'

But I was not alone in this. And we don't face up to these stories well. Consider the (then) prominent charismatic Anglican leader Mark Stibbe who in 1995 argues that the Toronto Blessing was the first sign of a 'fourth wave' of renewal which would result in global revival. Or consider Paul Cain who prophesied in July 1990 that a mighty revival would break out in London. He had been partly introduced in the UK via John Wimber by shining lights of the UK charismatic scene including Stibbe's predecessor at St Andrews Chorleywood David Pytches, the founder of New Wine, and Sandy Millar at HTB. They helped usher in the

Kansas City Prophets to the UK. John Wimber even declared that 'Cain was never wrong in his prophecies'.

The whole thing got out of hand.

These predictions were heightened with 'supra-biblical' teaching from Bob Jones, who Wimber had apparently endorsed as highly prophetic while acknowledging he had a 'demonic problem'. Jones promised a dramatic increase in signs of wonders for a 'new breed of men' and an 'army of locusts' who would sweep across the nation in a Holy Spirit revival.

The revival never came, and a few months later Wimber contracted cancer of the throat which stymied much of the rest of his ministry. His wife Carol's post-humous biography of John Wimber tells how many people tried to link his embracing of these prophetic ministries with his illness, but also tells of both of their regrets about endorsing Jones and Cain. Wimber died in 1997 and a year before he gave a retrospective to UK Vineyard leaders saying that:

"During the period of the 'prophetic era' [Kansas City Prophets] and on into the 'new renewal' [Toronto] our people quit starting small groups, they quit prophesying, they quit healing the sick, they quit casting out demons, because they were waiting for the Big Bang, the Big Revival, the Big Thing… *I thought, My God, we've made an audience out of them. And they were an army!*"[1] (John Wimber)

This was a huge admission from a champion of the charismatic movement, but we never talk about it. Using promises of hope made an audience out of an army. Will there

---

[1] Carol Wimber, 'John Wimber: The Way It Was.' N.P.: Independently Published, 1999. 179-181

ever be a day when charismatic leaders don't declare some out of context promise from Isaiah as heralding in a new day for their institution, or assert that the coming world revival won't begin in their town? Or when itinerant ministers will stop parodying British comic Michael Macintyre who declares wherever he goes that this is his 'favourite venue', when they declare wherever they go that this city will surely be revival HQ? If the mistakes of people as admirable as Millar, Pytches and Wimber led to an audience not an army, why do we imagine anything different from each new false dawn sold to willing dreamers?

We will return in later chapters to the misuse of truth, scripture and of power, but a word here is surely necessary about the platform.

In a flat church hierarchy where it is hard for ambitious and talented people to assess their own performance, and ecclesiastical promotion (preference) may be rare, the one sad scorecard available to ministers on a set stipend is their status on the speaking circuit. This can be an anaemic circuit made up of identikit performers touting their wares from a parade of platforms, pleasing with platitudes to a culture that celebrates celebrity. It's harder to break into than Major League Soccer (where no teams are promoted or relegated for poor performance).

 But it remains an illusory goal. It is why it was so moving a few years ago to hear a prominent speaker from Northern Ireland, Alan Scott, talk about how God wants people who want to get on an altar not a platform (based on the Romans 12 charge for us to be 'living sacrifices'). 'Make the sacrifice' he intoned from the platform he'd been flown in to occupy. And yet now we hear reports that he drove staff to conversion quotas and faces a lawsuit about the manner and way he has taken $66million worth of Anaheim Vineyard real estate out of the USA Vineyard network.

Get an altar not a platform. Good advice. But the reality is the great altar in the Old Testament was higher off the ground than a conference stage. Leaders are exposed. It's one thing to be a living sacrifice in private, quite another to do it in public. You don't even need to get off the altar to turn it into a stage. You just have to stand up and make it about you.

My goodness, the water has got murky.

But the bathwater needs flushing if the baby is to survive and grow.

Chapter Three:
Driven To Distraction By Success

Dear friends,

A few weeks ago, my near neighbour Giles Fraser hit several nails on their heads from the leafy London suburb of Kew when he launched a lament on success culture and 'entertainment church'. He describes a frenetic institution whose workers were unable to sit on their own in an empty room with only God for company, and a third of the clergy felt like quitting. A church infected by a secular age whose managers are addressing the wrong problems as they demand more innovation. It's worth a read if you're not too depressed already.

More recently Stephen Kneale has written a fascinating blog about the pendulum shift reaction against a driven culture in the church/society. This swing he argues has got us into a mess of a different sort:

"And where has that got us? In a place where it can be hard to motivate volunteers to do anything that is anything less than exactly what they desperately want to do because they enjoy it. A place where the hard graft of ordinary ministry just doesn't get done. A place where, if I'm not feeling it, I just don't do it. If I haven't had four nights in with my family, I'm really being pushed too hard. A place where the lost can go to Hell (quite literally) because I'm feeling a bit tired and need my "me time". Or, I don't go anywhere or do anything uncomfortable at all because I doubt I'll be fully glorifying God in my attitude when I find it at all difficult." (Stephen Kneale)

Some online memes suggest this is a generational issue. Boomers go off to work singing 'Hi Ho, Hi Ho, It's off to Work we Go'; Millennials chant 'You're welcome' to their boss who is expected to be thrilled they've turned up; and Gen Z shuffle in late to 'It's a Hard Knock Life for Us' if they feel like it. I'm sure it's far more nuanced than that, but the parody has the seed of something in it.

We are clearly living in an age in the church where some people have given up hope, some people have checked out early (while still taking a stipend/wage), some people have burnout, and some people feel like they and they alone are trying really hard here, and why won't everyone else join in?

It's easy to think that their stereotypes apply to the cooler kids down the road from you. But let's bring it closer to home:

Let's talk Success.

If you were talking to a mentor or spiritual director and they asked:

What does success mean to you?

What would you do to get success?

What would you do to sustain success?

Would it prick the conscience of your heart if you answered in bare honesty?

As I interviewed church leaders it became crystal clear that success is a validator for many of us.

It validates not just our job performance but our sense of being. It can become the air we breathe, the expectation that we have. Our way of measuring performance. Our way of measuring up to expectations others put on us or inspire in us.

Drivers

In the last chapter we talked about some of the messy bathwater around the beautiful baby that is the charismatic movement. A chunk of that touched on the need, desire or motivation for success. I've written at length about that motivation in my thesis and journeyed with the problem for at least 9 years. But this week I was away with our church staff team re-learning some old lessons about 'what is your driver' and came face to face with it for myself again.

A driver is a motivator that makes you do what you do. It may well be positive – there's no prize for doing nothing – but it will have with a shadow side to it. But from all the options Paul and Christine Perkin laid out I couldn't work it out what mine was until a day or two later when I was sitting at my desk reading the book of Hebrews.

The options were:

The drive to be **perfect** – we value success and achievement.

The drive to **please** others – we value peace at any price.

The drive for **efficiency** – we value activity and energy.

The drive to be **strong** – we value independence and courage.

The drive to **try** harder – we value effort and determination.

None quite fit in the session, although there were traces of all of them. In some ways I'd been battling with a few years of thesis / covid induced lethargy, burying whatever talents I may have had. I felt like I was just getting my drivers back and I valued them.

Then it hit me. And it was a shocker.

A driver on a par with the 'angel of light' himself when he fell like lightning from heaven.

An absolute scorcher of a needy driver.

It pains to admit it.

The driver to be praised. The driver to be exalted.

It's a bit different to the 'please others' driver. It's not about them coming near or keeping peace. It's about being praised from a distance. Being praiseworthy. Being seen as deserving of a place at the top table. It's not quite the same as valuing success. It is valuing that others value your success!

It's not hard to psychologise where it came from in my life. I grew up in a very high affirmation culture at home and then was over-promoted at junior school to 'head boy' (in a school where my dad was headmaster!) I remember the angst of not making the first round of prefects in my senior school where the electors were not trying to please my dad! This must have played into a deep need in me to show that I was good enough to get to the top. Not the top for a purpose. Not the top to do anything when up there. Just the top for the view. It all sounds shockingly Boris Johnson to me, but that may be unfair on the former British Prime Minister.

So how could this desire to be exalted still be bobbling up in me nearly 30 years after my conversion? How have I not received inner healing to my 'wounded child within'? How have I not put to death whatever remains of the sinful nature / been crucified with Christ? How have I not learnt to live out fully all the things I preach on?

I guess the answers are a mixed bag. There's a bit of me that wants to stand up on the altar we finished the last chapter with and get a whole bunch of praise. A bit of me that wants my big brother Jesus to get all the glory. A bit of me that loves having a perfect sibling. A bit of me that wants to compete. A bit of me that really, really wants other people to thank me – so I can get the double joy of 'humbly' deflecting it away to the 'glory of God'.

Living for the Praise of His Glory and a heavenly 'well done'.

Sometimes God is broadcasting a message to you. Have you ever found that? He keeps finding ways to say the same thing, until it sinks in.

A few days before the 'drivers' teaching I had been preaching on Galatians 1:10.

Am I now trying to win the approval of human beings, or of God? Or am I trying to please people? If I were still trying to please people, I would not be a servant of Christ.

St Paul, Galatians 1:10

I had clocked the negative, but not the positive.

I saw clearly that if we are trying to please people we can't be a servant of God. Pleasing people here could be through our abilities to pioneer, connect, create, nurture, protect or whatever our strengths may be. Pioneers may be trying to please a demanding dad (long dead even), nurturers trying to keep peace because they grew up in dysfunctional homes. There are all sorts of personality type versions of 'trying to please people' we can fall into.

What I didn't see was the 'trying to win the approval of God' bit.

That's the game shifter.

My heavenly ABBA is really willing to cheer me on. As we pray on 'stir up Sunday' he does want to 'stir up my will to bring forth the fruit of good works'.

The Collect

> Stir up, we beseech thee, O Lord, the wills of thy faithful people; that they, plenteously bringing forth the fruit of good works, may of thee be plenteously rewarded; through Jesus Christ our Lord. Amen.

My heavenly ABBA does want to praise me.

He does want me to grow in perfection. After all, that was Jesus' punchline on the Sermon on the Mount. Be 'telos' as your heavenly Father is 'telos' [telos = complete/perfect].

He does want me to be at peace with those around me and bring peace. 'Blessed are the peacemakers.'

He does want me to expend energy and actively bring the Kingdom on earth. As Paul puts it: "To this end I strenuously contend with all the energy Christ so powerfully works in me." (Col 1.29).

He does want me to grow in strength of mind, soul, body and spirit so that I can love him with all my heart, all my soul, mind and strength.

He does want me to try hard, to use the talents he has given me to their maximum, to run the race, to fight the fight…

He is sitting there in heaven with a great cloud of witnesses cheering me on.

He is delighting over me with singing as he was delighting over the people of Israel Zephaniah wrote to. My heavenly ABBA delights over me with singing.

He does want me to have a vision of His glory and does want me to have a vision of His church that would enable me 'for the joy set before me' to 'endure' whatever 'cross' he sends my way, just like my big brother Jesus did.

He does want to clothe prodigal Richard in a royal robe, and he does want to welcome me home to the sound of an Almighty party.

Why would I live for anything less?

Bursting the Bubble

Because it's easy to slip from the approval of God bit to enjoying the praise of people, I'm pretty sure God puts people around us to burst our bubble and give us a chance of surviving this narrow path spiritual walk. I've had a few of those bubbles burst over the years.

Paul knew something of this when he talked about a messenger of Satan being sent to him to burst his bubble after he had had some 'surpassing revelations' he realised he couldn't talk about. He called this messenger of Satan a thorn in the flesh. It was as irritant to remind him that we're not here to build up 'me'. Not to get buffed up. Not to take on the role of messiah. Not to seek human praise.

"If I were still trying to please people, I would not be a servant of Christ." Galatians 1:10

What a tragedy to climb some spiritual ladder of success and realise it was the very same ladder the angel of light Lucifer climbed before he fell from heaven.

What a trap, to build up our own movement only to realise the ladder that seemed to soar so high is hovering over the pit of hell, while the entrance to heaven was a narrow gate, an 'eye of the needle' best walked through on your knees.

I have been very blessed by a family who don't take me seriously, and plenty of people to challenge my path so far. A few who have painfully burst my bubble – both friends and foes – may have actually been sent to save me. It could have gone differently.

Driven or not?

We began with Giles Fraser's lament about driven freneticism and burnout and Stephen Kneale's observation that 'self-care' can slip into 'don't care'.

How about you?

You may have other drivers like the ones Paul and Christine Perkin shared with our church staff team that have got a bit out of kilter: Be perfect. Please others. Be efficient. Be strong. Try harder.

Or you may be uber passive. Given up on positive drivers and copped out of life, ministry and the good race.

Didn't want to get it wrong, so didn't have a go.

Didn't want to fail, so didn't try.

Didn't think you could, so quit before you started.

Ring any bells?

There are no prizes in heaven for not even trying to run the race.

Consider what Jesus said about the man with one talent, who buried it.

It's a stark warning not to be a quitter, a sulker or compare ourselves with others to the point of giving up.

But it really is a minefield isn't it. Does anyone get it right?

A church leader wrote to me after reading the last chapter. He said:

> "So many people walking on the street who I long to see come to Christ who we just haven't reached. 'Lord, how will we ever reach them – it's just too much! I give up, You are going to have to do it!' And then I paused and thought for a moment... Of course! It's only Him who can do anything; I can't turn someone to Jesus, I can't make them be born again; it's all Him. What in me, in

my tradition, leans me to think constantly (while I believe in the power of prayer) that it's about what I do, what we run, how active and engaged in the community we are that will lead people to Him. As you observed of Alpha – 'Alpha saved my life', we as church leaders may smile, but do we not fall into the trap of seeing the multitude of events, services, programmes and activities we run, being Messiah, and as we do, exhaust ourselves because we are the curators of these things? I'm not advocating nothing, inertia, but how do you stop Jesus' hands and feet dislocating themselves from the body and particularly the head?"

Church Leader

It's a good question, a great one to end on and ponder today.

CHAPTER FOUR:
WHOEVER PAYS THE PIPER

Dear friends,

There is a price for maintaining success.

There was a seminal moment at the New Wine summer festival in 2013 when Justin Welby (the newly appointed Archbishop of Canterbury) made his way back to the New Wine festivals he had attended incognito for years. He got on the main stage and said, 'The trouble with New Wineskins is they get older.'

> "Now, first of all, if you'll excuse me being quite impolite, the trouble with New Wineskins is that they get older. I'm looking around. I look in the mirror. It's a bit frightening. That may seem shocking and rude, but I'm afraid it's true, and it is the pattern of all renewal in the Church. As they get older, they accumulate bits and pieces that attach to them; they get baggage… New Wine has done much; has been a great channel of the grace of God; has changed and trained two generations of leaders. But we are in a time of revolution, and we need another revolution in the Church. What it looks like, I do not know, but I want to be in it. What it feels like is Jesus-centred, fire-filled, peace-proclaiming,

disciple-creating, and the Church word for this revolution is revival."

Justin Welby, 2013

He was effectively asking the poignant question: 'If you've been offering the same spiritual beverage for 25 years can it really be 'New Wine'?'

Choruses, conferences and courses – When does a Movement become a Monument?

It was a question that reverberated through the tent meeting, but did little to stop charismatics in the UK doing the same things and offering the same 'beverages' for the next six years. The only thing that broke the format of 'choruses, conferences and courses' was Covid-19. That is apart from a seemingly prescient Mike Pilavachi announcing that God had told him to stop the vastly influential festival 'Soul Survivor' just before the pandemic broke out.

Soul Survivor had been a youth spin-off from New Wine, a festival that also grew out of the Anglican church St Andrew's Chorleywood where Mike Pilavachi had been a youth worker. At its peak it attracted 25,000 teens and young adults a year. But stopping Soul Survivor just led to a plethora of rival youth conferences vying to take its place. The Anglican link though has been broken and with it the steady stream of young people from all denominational backgrounds who found themselves heading into Church of England ministry through Soul Survivor. Retrospectively you wonder if the 'prescience' was trustees/funders forcing him to shut it down as the whispers that crescendoed into a cacophony of accusations in 2023 became too much to bear.

We have to talk about money. Because we have to be able to answer one key question: Who are you yoked to in ministry?

Choruses

There is a lot that has been written about the impact of money on the Christian music scene – including on contemporary worship. When big record labels get a say in what gets promoted, pushed and produced they become the theological gatekeepers of our age. More theology is caught as we sing than taught as we listen. So just 5 or 6 Western churches become our marketable musical therapy factories, and we all sing along to their comforting tune. A movement that began with three chords and a rainbow guitar strap becomes a marketing machine.

But there are other 'yokings' that go on.

Conferences

As festivals get more expensive than the gate price can bring in, they too become a machine in need of sustaining. One approach is that industrial level charities with turnovers ten times bigger than the festival are invited to sponsor events in return for advertising space/time. The payback is promotion: Punters signing up as entry level donors for their charity. But this has to firstly cover the overheads of sponsoring the event, the fundraisers' salaries and other charity overheads, and then hopefully supporting the charity a little from any surplus. For the charities however this is a once-a-year opportunity at a captive audience and for their well remunerated fundraisers it's a no-brainer. Once hooked the hope is that the punters will i) move up their giving pyramid, ii) influence others to do the same and iii) ultimately leave endowments or iv) trigger a high-end donor to outgive everyone else there. (But if the industrial level charity has overheads of 40% and has an executive on $0.5 million a year, you have to wonder where all those monthly pledges are going).

On the other hand, all this can be carefully curated so that chosen charities align well with the event organisers' priorities. Indeed, just as when you watch Saturday night TV or a major sports broadcast sometimes the adverts can be more inspiring than the planned programme.

But the punters are in little doubt they are sitting through a commercial.

We move from:

Worship – Teaching – Ministry

to

Worship – Advert – Worship – Advert / Appeal – Teaching – Ministry…

… with worship carefully curtailed to make sure there is time for the adverts and appeals.

All this is to cover the expense / needs of the festival goers.

The show must go on.

Even in the once 'new wineskins' have been stretched out of shape.

Courses

Back in the late 1990s a question that was beginning to stir in missiologist and retired bishop Simon Barrington-Ward. Bishop Simon brought me into the Church of England. I was singing the praises of the Alpha Course to him, when he paused and said, 'yes, but really Richard, what comes next?'

Alpha's UK peak was probably 1998. By then many other missiologists were asking, 'What's next'. Few were predicting the reality: Alpha and more Alpha.

By the 21st Century Alpha was an enormous enterprise. A movement had become a machine. It had more employees than some dioceses, a turnover of £12 million a year and an international presence based on the assumption that a course designed for the upper middle-class sensibilities of the luxurious London district of Knightsbridge was marketable from Zurich to Zimbabwe. Like some of its spiritual cousins running conferences, publishing houses, or worship music labels it found it was a machine that needed sustaining by marketing. A key question was how long until it became a monument to something God was doing in the past? Were there echoes of Justin Welby's statement again? 'The trouble with new wineskins is they grow old.'

Yet in the meantime the minister 'down the road' at Westminster Chapel, RT Kendall, was prophetically warning in his 2004 classic book 'The Anointing' that the enemy of the next revival was likely to be the protagonists of the last one.

Could it be that the 1990s generation who had experienced the good and bad of the Toronto Blessing, but missed out on their expected world revival, have carried on propagating what they knew worked a bit, at the expense of what could have been far better?

Surely they knew with each passing year that the courses – conference – choruses mix was a pale reflection of 'the coming world revival' that had been promised in 1989?

Or has the question of when the machine would become a monument to a faded glory been ignored.

Many of these charismatic icons – courses, conferences and choruses – owe their origins to men who have had an anointing to reboot the church. These men began a ministry that became a movement. But inevitably those movements mechanise as they fight for air space, funding and profile. They can so easily become a monument to a past glory/man that we are too entwined with to disentangle from.

Yet it's one thing to be yoked with a wealthy funder who shares your values, or to propagate a course, conference or chorus style that you really believe in and know still works. But what happens when you get yoked to a national church whose vacillating values you (no longer) share?

Backing Justin: Queen Anne's Bounty

While the same spiritual beverage continued to be offered in the networks, right from the early days of his episcopacy the archbishop was making seismic waves in the institutional church. He was still seen in those days as 'someone we should back whatever he does'. At least that's how Nicky Gumbel put it from the platform of the Albert Hall at HTB's loss-leader Leadership Conference. This rally call to back 'Justin' was echoed by other networks. The early Welby-era was a golden age for charismatics in the institution.

Under Archbishop Justin Welby, tens of millions of pounds of central and diocesan Church of England funds would be released to start identikit HTB style network churches around the country. Funding and training would be provided through the Gregory Centre for Church Multiplication led by one-time HTB associate vicar Ric Thorpe and by the new 'St Mellitus College', a vicar factory that let students continue to serve in their network church for the bulk of their training. Bishops were appointed, persuaded or funded into getting with the programme. A church planting movement had been unleashed on the C of E.

Church Multiplication

The results were staggering. Potential growth in network churches soon outstripped even HTB's £12 million a year budget and negotiations were made to get more church planting curates funded by the central Church of England. While HTB paid in just £250,000 a year into diocesan funds, dozens of curates were centrally funded on stipend-housing-pension packages, to serve and learn at the multisite London campus and take their franchise around the country.

When bright eyed planters arrived at a new location, they received funding for 3-5 years. This might mean up to 5 staff members (vicar, associate, operations, worship, youth children's worker) and building improvements that could reach further millions of pounds of funding. The revolution had begun, but so had the countdown to replace the funding. It took a new breed of self-confident clergy to imagine they could grow a church in 3-5 years sufficiently to continue to fund all those roles. Not many had taken an honest assessment of how often you need a nearby church/churches to implode to achieve the rapid growth the model demanded.

As the planting spiralled other movements/churches were welcomed as the protagonists of planting looked to broaden their appeal. This was key to gain legitimacy with the bureaucratic 'checks and balances that be' within the C of E and keep the cash flowing. Funding spread to New Wine churches, Conservative CoMission/Re:New churches and any central/catholic churches who could be persuaded to join in, most notably St Martin's in the Fields with their HeartEdge project. All were equally happy to take Queen Anne's Bounty.

The Price of the Piper

For evangelicals in the Church of England a massive shift has occurred in the funding model. In the early 2000s most medium/large evangelical churches were autonomous self-funding churches, net contributors to their diocese, happily on the edge, and often with 'patronage' vested in evangelical agencies who would help appoint new vicars when there was a vacancy. Patronage was the legacy of earlier church planters like Charles Simeon who established or bought many now famous churches in such a way that trustees should be able to ensure evangelical succession whatever the theological whim of the Diocese or national church. Simeon's legacy includes: St Aldate's Oxford, Trinity Cheltenham, Christ Church Clifton and Christ Church Winchester – fruit that has lasted centuries. But for a relatively small amount of seed money many established parishes have given over their autonomy for start-up salary grants or the chance to become a resource church, and purpose planted resource churches are beholden to their diocese in a way that would make Charles Simeon squirm. Expect future job adverts for City Centre Resource Churches to read between the lines: 'Wanted, tame evangelical-ish minister, who likes dressing down and guitar music, to fit into our diocesan 'strategy' and values, and be nice to the bishop.' How many will leave a legacy that lasts to a second or third generation?

Meanwhile in a national church desperate not to dissolve, opportunities abound for charismatics with some track record of success. A form of charismatic practice has become a new normal in the Church of England as 'tame evangelical-ish' prelates proliferate. But as with funding, the price of promotion is aligning yourself to an institution that is a machine not a movement. Some can rise above that. Others unwittingly validate the joke that a consecration is the spiritual removal of a backbone by fellow bishops. For many though even an elusive promise of preferment means that happens several stages earlier. A million little career choices not to be 'dangerously radical'. A million ways to conform to church not to Christ. And while most who may not even gain the whole (ecclesiastical) world, many are prepared to run the gambit of forfeiting their soul.

Churches are now yoked to dioceses and the national church in a new way.

Charismatics have never had so much favour, opportunities or preferment. Never had so much money being thrown their way in stipends, grants, church plants… Never had so many institutions of their own that need to be sustained. They've accumulated conferences, courses, bishops and archbishops and got baggage by the bucket load.

But what will be the cost, and what has been the cost already?

Chapter Five:
Losing My Religion? Evangelical-Ish

Dear friends,

I came across a book review this week that laments:

Many theologians are introducing revisions into the classical doctrine of God. This revisionist work is occurring not only among mainline theologians but among evangelical and even Reformed theologians as well.

Review of James Dolezal, *All That Is In God* By Keith Mathison

In summary Mathison argues

> "The contemporary departures from classical Christian theism are no minor matter. These doctrines are influencing the next generation of pastors who will, in turn, fill the pulpits of the church. This is why it is important that those in the pews of these churches be aware of what is going on and be able to recognize departures from historical biblical orthodoxy when they see it. If one does not understand the biblical grounds for the classical doctrine, the arguments made by the revisionists can seem plausible and persuasive. Take the

time to learn why these doctrines have been the heritage
of the church for thousands of years."

Keith Mathison

To be honest that's about all of the review I really understood.
The pros and cons of theistic mutalism, impassiblity, and
divine simplicity which each get a chapter in Dolezal's book
seem beyond most things I have studied in three theology
degrees, and not common dinner table discussions here in the
UK. We'll come back to why that may be in the next chapter.

But the conclusion is a familiar theme to me. A generational
slide.

A large chunk of my thesis has been on a generational shift in
doctrine.

Feeding the Beast

It became interesting to me when I met with Sandy Millar in
2017. He'd kindly invited me out to Suffolk to discuss both
my writing and a parish weekend he was going to take for
Christ Church W4. We got to talking about Alpha and the
HTB network. He gave me a well-rehearsed line, which I later
found out was also quoted by Monica Furlong, in her 2000
book *The Church of England: The State it is In,* p.274. The line
was:

'We need to change the model, not the message.'

In Furlong's book Millar elaborates:

'The trouble with the Church of England is that as the
market is distancing itself from us we have been forced
to change either the message or the model.'

Sandy Millar

Millar states that changing the message is a 'total failure' as the market hopes to hear that the church 'actually does believe in something'. Rather it is the model that needs changing, to connect with the young.'

It sounds so simple. Change the packaging. Enhance production values. Boost the presentation. Keep the age-old message the same. And Sandy has been brilliant at communicating it.

But a lingering question remained as I heard this: Is it possible to change the model without changing the message? Which parts of the message get accentuated in the changed model? Do any parts get dropped?

A further question I reflected on years later is about 'the market'.

Is the market something neutral? Do Christians simply need to discern market demand and then supply a felt need? If the need is purpose, supply a 'life worth living now'. If the need is connection, supply a 'relationship with Jesus'. If the need is spirituality, supply a tangible 'encounter with the Holy Spirit' in a contained course setting.

But what if it's not simply neutral? Could 'giving the market what it wants' feed a consumerist beast? What if that beast then outgrows its cage if it has too much to feast on?

What if the beast doesn't want to hear the whole counsel of God? Would the model have changed the message then?

Mind the Gap

The reality is that presenting the gospel in a more attractive, winsome and even edited way doesn't necessarily change the message. Not the message you think you believe anyway.

My thesis explores the emerging gap between what we think we believe, what we say we believe in public and what an outsider could discern we believe by watching us and listening to us.

What we believe is the **normative** theology – the key sources texts, influences and doctrines we hold dear. The 'hill we would die on' in years gone by. This can stay the same even if you edit what you say in public.

What we say we believe is **espoused** theology. It differs from normative theology if we don't teach our core beliefs systemically or we let other ideas come in and take up airtime / head space.

What others can discern is **operant** theology – our theology in practice, which can be syncretised with any cultural winds and waves that surround us.

So our message can be exactly the same as it was in our normative theology. Our core beliefs. The books, teachers, authors, creeds and source texts we turn to. But if you listened to us and / or observed us it might have changed a whole lot.

There is a sign on the back of the London Red Buses at the moment. It's for careful driving. It says: 'Watch Your Speed Your Son Does'.

The advertisers know that I might have a normative theology of driving that says, '20 miles an hour in an urban setting is sensible road safety.' I may have an espoused theology of driving that says to my son 'slow down for speed bumps and crossings'. But if I have an operant theology of driving where I excuse myself for speeding generally, my son is going to pick up my habits and excuses not my unspoken and undemonstrated beliefs.

Changing the model (and the message) has led to an increasing gap between normative, espoused and operant theologies in many of our charismatic churches. This happens when there is little/no attempt to pass on the normative theology. When normative theology is taken for granted, not contended for.

And that means the next generation starts from a new place.

They start from what they have seen and heard.

They start from the marketing.

The lost message?

In my thesis I explore three ancestors of the UK charismatic Anglican scene. Three people/eras with whom you might expect us to share DNA if you know our history.

Closest up: John Wimber

Further back: A surprise entry for some – John Stott.

Historical Mirror: John Wesley and George Whitefield.

Wimber

We'll explore Wimber's impact in later chapters but for now I want to zoom in on his theology.

Don Williams, a theologian operating within the Vineyard movement, gives a useful summary. He sees Wimber not as a modernist and therefore not a fundamentalist either and that he was more like a pre-modernist than a postmodern. Hence, he was at home in the age that dominated the church and the West before the Enlightenment, inspired by the likes of the miracle performing St Cuthbert. This meant he was able to position the 'Vineyard' to bring a spiritual reality to the 'emerging antimodern ethos of the emerging postmodern age'.

For Williams, Vineyard under Wimber was strongly evangelical theologically, but 'surprisingly open', and influenced particularly by five movements in history.

The Vineyard Statement of Faith draws on these five movements spanning church history: 1) the Patristic Period – which gives it a Trinitarian orthodoxy; 2) the Reformation – underlining the sufficiency of Christ alone, and the final authority for the written Word of God 'separating the Vineyard from neoorthodoxy and liberal evangelicalism'; 3) the Eighteenth-Century Great Awakening – emphasizing new birth, conversion, regeneration and a life of holiness 'personal sanctification'; 4) the modern missionary movement – driving back the kingdom of Satan by evangelization; 5) the biblical theology movement – essentially George Ladd's Kingdom Theology that was taught at Fuller Seminary.

John Stott

In my thesis I argue that John Stott is the 'forgotten father' to HTB providing the foundations for its orthodox growth in the 1980s and 1990s. John Collins would often say "All my theology is Stott's", with a wistful, but still loyal, lament at the unwanted gap that developed between him and his mentor from 1963 over the charismatic movement.

As David Edwards put it, John Stott:

"Consistently taught a religion which claims to be true and not merely enjoyable or useful; which asks people to think, not merely to tremble or glow; which bases itself on a book which can be argued about, not on experience which convinces only the individual who has had it."[1]

Traditionally evangelicals in the Church of England were quite easy to spot. According to David Bebbington they were marked by four operant, espoused and normative distinctives which Timothy Dudley Smith says Stott epitomised.

People of the **cross** – 'crucicentric' – who saw the cross as the centre of their faith.

People of the **Bible** – 'biblicist' – who saw the bible as living, powerful and sharper than a double-edged sword.

People of **conversion** – 'conversionist' – who emphasised the need to be born again, die to sin and be transformed.

People of **activity** – 'activist' – who were inspired by stories such as the speech of condemned criminal Charles Peace who was escorted on the gallows by a prison chaplain reading about the fires of hell. Peace burst out.

"Sir, if I believed what you and the church of God say that you believe, even if England were covered with broken glass from coast to coast, I would walk over it, if need be, on hands

---

[1] Edwards, "Power of The Gospel," In David L. Edwards And John Stott, Evangelical Essentials (Downers Grove, Il: Intervarsity, 1989), 16.

and knees and think it worthwhile living, just to save one soul from an eternal hell like that!"[1]

Evangelicals were those with bloodied knees.

But none of these are very easy to market.

But that is our heritage.

Wesley and Whitefield

Finally for a historical mirror I bring together two men that have often been pitted against each by their followers (and at times by themselves), but who had a core 'teleology' in common.

In essence I argue their message was **'a holy people for a holy God.'**

A key dividing point between them was the extent to which holiness can be achieved in this life. But consider their similarity on the theme:

John Wesley believed that Charles and he had been called to propagate Christian holiness: 'holiness was our point – inward and outward holiness'. Again, with great clarity, he wrote to one of his preachers: 'Full sanctification is the grand depositum which God has lodged with the people called Methodists; and for the sake of propagating this chiefly he appears to have raised us up.'

Whitefield is well known for taking issue with Wesley's doctrine of Perfect Love. Yet despite the significant differences in early Methodism a clear discipleship goal of holiness was at the fore for both in their teaching and personal motivation.

[1] Ravenhill, Leonard (1987) [1959]. Why Revival Tarries. Bloomington, Mn: Bethany House Publisher. Pp. 33–34

Whitefield and Wesley were preparing holy people for a holy God to live in a holy eternity. Whitefield argued fervently that to be a Christian is "to be holy as Christ is holy" and that "Jesus Christ came down to save us, not only from the guilt, but also from the power of sin."

He himself confessed sin had no dominion over him, although he felt "the struggles of indwelling sin day by day." He even proclaimed that a mark of receiving the Holy Ghost is, "Not committing sin . . . This expression does not imply the impossibility of a Christian's sinning … It only means thus much; that a man who is really born again of God doth not willfully commit sin, much less believe in the habitual practice of it."

Consider also their key doctrines:

Wesley's have been helpfully summarised as follows: i) Scripture as 'the only standard of truth' ; ii) Salvation by faith as 'the standing topic' iii) sin as 'loathsome leprosy' ; iv) the regeneration through the Spirit by which we may be 'properly said to live' ; v) assurance as 'an inward impression on the soul' ; vi) holiness, 'the grand depositum'; vii) a desire to 'flee from the wrath to come' as the 'one condition' required of those wanting admission to the societies.

In an alternative scheme Outler picks just three: i) original sin, ii) justification by faith alone and iii) holiness of heart in those who have been born again.

Whitfield's focus was similar: 'the big truths of the Book of Truth', summarised by Maddock as 'original sin, justification by faith and the new birth' (although he notes the 'subtle but highly significant theological differences' and hence pastoral applications, that flow from Wesley and Whitefield's varying usage of identical terms).

Have we changed the model and the message?

Every generation needs to 'proclaim afresh' the good news. But when does marketing the gospel change the message? Or is the issue not so much marketing but a pendulum swing – a reaction to the former things – such as we often see in the church.

Many Anglican evangelicals touched by renewal in the 1960s onwards had lived with a legacy of teaching on holiness that was austere. It was often marked more by enforced abstinence from external markers deemed to be sinful (dancing, make-up, theatre, ornamentation) than by joy and victory. Once they experienced renewal, they were keen to avoid anything that seemed like a return to legalism after their own personal charismatic encounters. In the interviews a key HTB insider described what he saw as a common HTB metaphor for this change, as quoted in Chapter One:

Imagine carrying a backpack called Law for many years, then taking it off, eating the heavy food inside it and finding that what had been a burden on your back sustains you when eaten inside you.

As he describes it this led HTB increasingly to believe that it was the Spirit who changed behaviour, and gradually led to less ethical teaching about specific types of prohibited behaviour:

It became clear that we saw the Holy Spirit working in people's lives to change people from the inside rather than say 'you've got to live like this'. And so, there's been a subtle shift over time where [HTB] will still say 'this is the way to live' but there won't be that 'stop doing this, stop doing that'. Just much more 'follow the Spirit and let Him convict you'.

In other words, stop teaching the hard stuff – the Holy Spirit will remind you of that when you need it. Preach the positives.

It's not hard to see how that colludes with marketing the message.

And shifts the message.

And how over a generation or two the message shifts.

Because the only thing you can be 'reminded' of is something you have been taught.

Evangelical-ish

My hot take on Bebbington's Quadrilateral is that only one of these four points is still seen in much of the contemporary charismatic church.

Crucicentric has been replaced with a (therapeutic) experience of the Spirit.

Biblicist has been put through the prism of positivity so much that the bible becomes a self-help manual (where referred to).

Conversionist has been subbed off the pitch and replaced with 'a relationship with Jesus' which in a swipe left/swipe right era means little more than 'until it's no longer working for me'.

Activist remains, although post-covid there's a notable upturn in what Catherine Tate called 'Am I bovvered'. The biggest call is comfort.

Of course, there are many who celebrate the change in the message. Looking for a connecting conversation with the century we live in, they are happy to palletise the prose, to dilute the doctrine, to preach the positives.

But others have ended up here accidentally. The idea that we preach a different gospel to Wesley, Whitefield, Stott or Wimber (wherever you want to place the mirror) is a wake-up call.

But we don't have to remain tame evangelical-ish… we can look to the rock from which we were hewn and really think…

THINK!

If we have accidentally, unwittingly changed the message, if a gap has emerged between what we think we believe, say we believe and seem to believe, if a generational shift has occurred because we've only passed on what we believed were the 'positives,' if we have self-edited ourselves and the gospel, if we have become 'caged birds'…

We have to think…

is it too late to look to the rock from which we were hewn…?

Or can we reconnect with our roots?

Chapter Six:
Spiralling Out Of Control | Caged Birds

Dear friends,

Last week we looked at whether you could change the model not the message. In this chapter we look at two reasons that the message has been more directly changed by charismatics.

I'm reminded of those nineteenth century intellectual iconoclasts who wanted to defend the gospel by editing away all the miracle stories. Their world had changed. A modernist worldview prevailed. Everything around them was being given a materialistic explanation. There was not much room for mystery, and the church's teaching seemed out of date or just plain unlikely to them.

To proclaim afresh the gospel to their generation in this context was hard.

What to do?

These iconoclasts set about finding anything in the gospels or Old Testament that had a miraculous base and gave it a sociological, phenomenological or materialist explanation. The Red Sea was parted by a random wind. Mass hysteria and hallucinations accounted for others. The bible was made into myth every time the hand of heaven touched earth.

Why?

Because their worldview didn't allow for the miraculous. They felt they had to put the whole thing into a box if they were going to sell it to their peers and to themselves. Schliermacher considered that the significance of a miracle "lies not in the means by which it occurs, whether natural or supernatural, but in its source and in the message or feeling that it is able to evoke". He denied that there is any "supernatural" reality alongside "natural" reality, and it therefore becomes meaningless to designate some events as "supernatural."

This theory played out in all sorts of ways until two centuries later I encountered it in a URC Sunday School as a teenager. The teacher wanted to make faith more palatable for us and tried persuading us that the miracle of the loaves and fishes multiplying was a miracle of human generosity. A generous boy shared food, which triggered previously hungry families to remember they too could share. Both Schliermacher and my aging teacher wanted to reduce my barriers to belonging to the Christian faith. As a modernist I might have been grateful, but this was the 1990s, the cusp of a post-modern age where we were not intellectually bound to simple solutions, and anyway I had been brought up on missionary stories of multiplication in all sorts of settings. I walked out at the end of the class and never returned to the crumb of hope he was trying to share.

These days we are not likely to edit away the miraculous. Culture has shifted and post-modern and pre-modern spirituality (such as Wimber's) is in vogue. We are happier with the idea that materialism can't explain it all. Miracles are back in. But culturally we have plenty of other issues with the Christian faith. There will always be a market for a culturally relevant edit to the gospel even if, as with Schliermacher, the edit changes the whole thing.

It's ironic that at the end of the story that Sunday School teacher was trying to make palatable the crowd deserts Jesus. In a single chapter of John's gospel Jesus goes from Mega-Church pastor to small group leader. It is one of the most scandalous examples of 'church decline' in the history of Christianity. Only Peter and the small band of devoted followers remain.

Why did they stay?

Because despite hard and divisive teaching that has lost him a vast crowd Jesus 'has the words of eternal life'. His message that 'unless you eat the flesh of the Son of Man and drink his blood, you have no life in you' may be exclusivist, challenge the known world order and seem intolerant, but Peter argues 'to who else will we turn.'

Peter had come to 'believe and to know' that Jesus is 'the Holy One of God'. To whom else could he turn? I guess in that context he felt ill-equipped to demand Jesus toned it down a bit.

As we preach a Christ who could lose a crowd just as easily as he could draw one, we might find it a little strange to think how much we're prepared to shift his message today in the vague hope that we will hold on to a crowd, congregation, or culture of our own.

Spiralling out of Control

Someone recently described to me meeting a very senior church figure here in the Church of England not long after he had been hauled in front of some parliamentary noteworthies. Not long in post his bubble burst already. He looked ashen and curtowed by their agenda. The threat was to take away the Church of England's standing in the world. The unstated cost of retaining the whole world? His very soul. Or at least that's the dichotomy Jesus warned about in Mark 8 if we seek to cling on to all that is here. His response. I'm going to do everything possible to make sure we don't lose world on my watch.

Secular comedians have long labelled the Church of England as a spineless enterprise. Eddie Izard's 'Cake or Death' sketch is a classic.

(www.youtube.com/watch?v=rZVjKlBCvhg&t=110s)

The Yes, Minister series had a compelling sketch on choosing a bishop.

Three punchlines echo through the sketch:

"When they stop believing in God, they call themselves a modernist."

"Theology is a device for enabling agnostics to stay in the church."

"I think God is what's called an optional extra."

But we laugh and chuckle and think that cannot be quite us. Even if it looks like an apt description from outside, we need some intellectual armour to persuade ourselves we're not quite as complicit as all that.

Rising above it all

Speaking truth to power has always been a costly thing, but what if we could avoid it?

What if there was a philosophical way of understanding the world that enabled a leader to say one thing to one group and another to another without feeling open to the charge of duplicity? What if you could elevate above other worldviews trapped in their limited understanding and reach enlightenment beyond? From such heights you could descend to groups with 'lower levels of consciousness' and talk to them in their language and terms and talk to other groups on other levels in their language and terms.

To the conservatives you sound conservative.

To the progressives you sound progressive.

To both, you give just a hint of 'knowing more than you do'.

To both, you give off a 'trust me I've got this and can see further than you can right now' vibe.

Welcome to the world of Spiral Dynamics

Spiral Dynamics is at first glance a pleasing leadership module popularised in Church of England circles by leadership guru Jim McNeish. McNeish is an effortlessly charming, charismatic communicator, who has headlined various leadership development programmes in the Church of England and charismatic networks. He has been a key trainer on the Church of England leadership pathways (for senior and strategic development) and mentored some prominent charismatics. He described himself as Justin Welby's leadership coach to the first cohort of the Strategic Leadership

Development Programme that has churned out a dozen or more of our current bishops.

Recently McNeish has hit the Christian Press as a key influence behind an alleged bullying practice at the (mini)megachurch Causeway Coast Vineyard. According to the Roys Report Senior Pastor Alan Scott used McNeish's Bioenergetics teaching (a Jungian based idea that body types equate to personalities) to hire and fire.

Back on the leadership programme McNeish described Justin Welby (to people handpicked to hang on to the archbishop's coattails) as a 'Yellow Leader'. The Yellow Leader is basically someone who has elevated beyond old certainties and even old questions, rising above conservatives and enlightened revisionists alike. From the Yellow viewpoint on the spiral, you can survey all you see and have a perspective lesser mortals can't cope with. But crucially you are not stuck in a superior ivory tower on the hill. As a Yellow Leader you can take the 'be all things to all men' and put it on steroids. You can go up and down the spiral at will and whether you are talking to a 'blue', 'green' or 'purple' meme person you can sound like you agree with them on everything. You speak their truth, their way and (because you have climbed the mountain and have a higher viewpoint) you call or nudge them upwards a little where you can.

You go to Africa and say one thing.

You go to parliament and say another thing.

You meet activists from various pressure groups in back-to-back meetings and spin on a circle.

You rise above it all, until a social media age questions how the guy we met in Ghana can have given that speech at Synod.

Spiral Dynamics is ultimately a gnostic dream. A dream that there is a level of enlightenment and superiority I can attain to that takes me beyond the simple, divisive truth of the man who said: 'unless you eat my flesh.' Like all gnostic dreams it is based on unreality and when it starts to tumble down it is terrible.

I spent a year trying to persuade my supervisors at Durham University to take Spiral Dynamics seriously, so I could use it as a conversation partner in my thesis. Maybe it could explain how we evolved as a network I thought, maybe we are leaving behind childish things, maybe this is what 'changing the model not the message' means, finding ways to talk to later-modern people while offering 'cake or cake'. But the more I looked into it the more disturbing its roots got, and flimsier the evidence for it was. They begged me to take it out for my own good. Not even academically credible as a conversation partner. A distraction from the main thing. Interesting for podcast aficionados and leadership seminars but not a rock to build your life on.

Within the Church of England this sort of thinking has produced an Orwellian nightmare of the most grotesque proportions. Bishops stand up and say black is white and white is black and expect us to swallow the poison. Bishops see themselves as a 'centre of unity' who can speak to all levels of the spiral, but get a headache when you put all the levels in the same room because they have to talk in three or four directions at once. Bishops who have forgotten that their job is defend the faith once given, not to reach a 'higher level of consciousness' that would give the Buddha altitude sickness.

Within the charismatic church I imagine it has had an effect too. We're well known for chasing after dreams, and visions. Paul had to tell his most charismatic church to keep their feet on the ground. It plays into our sense of superiority over conservative colleagues. We've got an extra level of revelation than you. A second blessing. A foot on a ladder even if that may be up the wrong wall. A way of relating to others in the wider church while we climb up to our own promotion position. But the wall came tumbling down on Babel's tower and will on this too. (Incidentally and somewhat ironically if you wanted to put Wimber on the Spiral he would be a 'level of consciousness' below the conservatives, as he embraced a pre-modern miracle working spirituality such as had characterised the Celtic saints).

Preaching the Positives

More briefly I want to mention some of the ways in which our responsiveness to perceived culture today can change our message. This is written up in far more detail in my thesis, links available at the end.

The essence is this: If we communicate that Christianity is a 'live worth living' (our 1990s charismatic mantra), and locate that 'worth living' in the here and now, and if we apply our teaching to give people tangible benefits right now, then eventually our focus will narrow to the point that we have left out big bits of our message so regularly and so often that they don't remain big bits of our message anymore.

Instead of giving a framework that produces a 'holy people for a holy God', instead of making an army (to use John

Wimber's phrase), we make an audience who drink the soothing Kool-Aid we supply. Feeling low? God want to raise you up. Feeling blue? God wants to comfort you. Feeling lonely? God wants to place you in a family. It's mass therapy, without doing what a therapist really should do… looking at where you have come from and where you are going. Somehow those two end points of faith have got lost. Our original sin and our eternal destiny(ies) are missing from the story, as are the consequences of living like a rescued redeemed people in amazement and gratitude at our salvation, and living as those who know a Day is coming where judgment will fall.

More so, we have also produced preachers who are caged birds. The image comes from China. Their authorised churches have certain books and themes they cannot preach from because government officials are looking on and censor them under threat of death or imprisonment. So their 'free' counterparts in the underground church call them caged birds.

Here our charismatic church is so domesticated you can leave the cage door open. We fly in all by ourselves and stay to 'preach the positives' in the hope that this will remove barriers of entry to others. The nightingale cry luring others into the cage too. You can read more in my thesis, but as we began to see in the last chapter the impact on generations is staggering. If you don't teach the whole counsel of God, but just a truncated 'me-orientated' scheme, the next generation only have a 'me-orientated' religion to chew on – or swallow like babies' milk.

Dear friends, some of our best communicators have preached the positives and got many into the gateway of the Kingdom of Heaven. God has used our networks greatly. But as we now see things spiralling out of control above us now is the time to ask the questions… were we climbing up the right hill anyway? Is theology being used all around us to hide atheism/ agnosticism or even something sinister? Why did Jesus choose death over cake (bread) in Matthew 4 and beyond…?

Is it time to rise up and lead people from the gateway into the whole counsel of God. To burst out of the cages and preach the truth unencumbered by a need for popularity or the winsomeness of the world. Is it time to say you can keep the world (and the world's grip on the church) but give me Jesus?

Chapter Seven:
Look To The Rock From Which You Were Cut

Dear friends,

A quick google search will give you all sorts of reasons to study, be aware of or be suspicious of history. Churchill telling us that 'history will be kind to me because I intend to write it', Martin Luther King Jr giving a far less power-based assessment: 'We are not the makers of history, we are made by history.' But even as Churchill had a sense of wanting to control the narrative, so he also drew on philosopher George Santayana who said

"Those who cannot remember the past are condemned to repeat it."

God in the Bible is often encouraging his people to historical recollection. In an antidote to Paul's 'forgetting what is past' passage, God, in Isaiah 51, shouts out to his people:

> *"Listen to me, you who pursue righteousness*
> *and who seek the Lord:*
> *Look to the rock from which you were cut*
> *and to the quarry from which you were hewn;*

look to Abraham, your father,
and to Sarah, who gave you birth."

Yet we've all known churches and people who are stuck in the past. Within charismatic renewal you can find churches that are temples to the 1960s/70s; others that are mementos to the Wimber years, and a few carpeted tabernacles to Toronto. There are even some which have a revolving altar pointing towards whichever place on the map is newsworthy at the moment within revivalist spheres. Helpfully, these are usually in North America – Brownville, Lakeland, Ashbury etc so the wheels on the altar don't need too much greasing.

But while God doesn't want us to be swept along by every fad that comes our way, nor does he want us to be stuck in the past. Paul is clearly right to 'press on to what is to come', and not get stuck reliving a series of anecdotes about 'when I was in Corinth/Ephesus/Antioch etc'.

So why does God encourage his people to look back to Abraham, Sarah et al? Why enshrine in his people's very calendar physical acts of remembrance, such as the feast of tabernacles, when they acted out living in the wilderness, or the Passover, when they remembered the great escape from Egypt? Why step into history at all, in the incarnation, and then ask us to 'remember' him at a time and place that would seem increasingly alien to his growing scattered people as the centuries go by?

I want to suggest three reasons why we in the infant charismatic church should at this point in our development engage with history:

- To know where we have come from – and hold up a mirror to where we are now.
- To know where we are going – and check that that is onto over a cliff hidden to us as we gaze at our toes.
- To hear the encouragement of the Hebrews 11 'great cloud of witnesses' and Revelation 6 and Revelation 20 martyrs, cheering us on and crying out to God 'how long' on our behalf. To realise that we are part of a marvellous church mystical as well as part of whatever small or large fellowship we may stumble into on a Sunday.

The Mirror

In my thesis I point to Wesley, Whitefield, Stott and Wimber as antecedents of the contemporary charismatic church, each in different ways, and simply ask: do we still believe, speak and act in a way that is congruent with them? Where there is a gap is that because we have evolved a higher level of understanding, or because we have truncated their scheme of salvation into something simpler, more immediately applicable or frankly easier.

Of course you have to be careful with this.

I first studied Wesley when I was a 19- and 20-year-old undergraduate. In a first draft of a thesis, submitted to the longsuffering and quite wonderful Brian Stanley, I began with words to the effect of:

In the 18th century England was spiritually moribund and so God raised up John Wesley.

Leaving aside the use of the word 'moribund' which I had just stumbled upon, Dr Stanley rightly suggested that my level of critical analysis would struggle to scrape a third-class degree. I rewrote it all in a week or so, and it was far better for it. The reality was the more I looked into Wesley, Whitefield or reformers like Luther, Calvin or later tried to make sense of the little we really know about the Celtic Saints, the more I had the same feeling I had when I started to read Genesis each year. In Genesis I 'looked to the rock from which I was hewn, Abraham your father and Sarah who gave you birth', and came away decidedly unimpressed. In the history books I had to grapple with Whitefield as a narcissistic 'divine dramatist', Wesley as a polemicist riding 19,000 miles partly to get away from his wife, Luther as an angry depressive, Calvin as an instrument of human power and control. All with an inspiring faith. But couldn't I just look at Jesus?

No one is perfect.

But that's the interesting thing about Christianity. It doesn't come in the form of a tract. A propositional truth. A two ways to live, a bridge to life, a 12 week course on key questions you may have. It comes in the form of a story.

His story.

History.

History of humanity.

History of a people chosen from humanity.

History of a person born into humanity.

History of a new humanity birthed out of an old humanity.

His story of what will happen at the end of history…

It is all immersed in history.

And a lot of the lessons are seen in the mess.

Yesterday I went to a parents evening at school. As the teacher described my son, I had a flash of self-recognition. Of course, I want and hope that he will be a better version of me having enhanced his gene pool so admirably by marrying well. But I kept getting flashes of 'I was just like that at his age' or (more worryingly perhaps) 'I am still like that too'.

We are born into history. It's very hard to make sense of ourselves outside of it.

History is there partly to show us that 'no temptation has seized you except what is common to people' and that 'God is faithful and will always give you a way to stand under such temptation.'

As with the famous Johari window, the more we know our church history, the more we know ourselves. Who we are. Where we come from. When we may have wandered off course.

Sometimes we will look in the mirror and see a family resemblance and smile. 'I've got my father's eyes.' 'John Wesley/Wimber/Collins would cheer this on.' Sometimes we look in the mirror and see a darker side, that history helps us spot. A cowardice moment reminiscent of father Abram in Egypt, a laugh/lie combo that reminds us of Mother Sarai. A narcissistic sneer, an angry turn, a self-absorption.

The more we look in the mirror at our spiritual family tree the more likely we are to avoid these pitfalls and stand on the shoulders of giants rather than have them fall on us.

Trajectory

We look back partly to check we are walking ahead well.

Imagine you got to have a supervision session with a saint from the past. St Brigid, Theresa of Avila, Florence Nightingale, Jean Darnell… whoever comes to mind. What would they ask you to cut to the core? What perspective would they bring to your 21st Century mind, heart, soul? Would you look them in the eye as they looked around your spiritual life and home?

There was an old China Inland Mission hymn with these words:

We bear the torch that flaming
Fell from the hands of those
Who gave their lives proclaiming
That Jesus died and rose
Ours is the same commission
The same glad message ours
Fired by the same ambition
To Thee we yield our powers

But we also remember the words of the Venite, Exultemus Dominus [Psalm 95] which the Church of England Common Worship brackets to encourages us to miss out:

Today if ye will hear his voice, harden not your hearts:
as in the provocation,
and as in the day of temptation in the wilderness;
When your fathers tempted me:
proved me, and saw my works.
Forty years long was I grieved with this generation, and said:

It is a people that do err in their hearts,
for they have not known my ways.
Unto whom I sware in my wrath
that they should not enter into my rest

In other words, history can get us thinking: am I on track (which sounds costly), or off track (which sounds calamitous).

Don't be like the desert forefathers. But do be like the desert fathers and other martyrs near God's throne.

But finally – I believe in the communion of saints

I want to finish with something completely different. What if we are not just talking about history in this chapter, but a living and ongoing present reality.

What if we are talking about the communion of saints. The church mystical. The cloud of witnesses and cry of heaven's martyrs.

What if these redeemed, once fallen, now exalted 'heroes of history' are really doing what the book of Hebrews claims and they are cheering us on?

You may have more or less theological issues with that depending on what you think happens to people who have died in the time leading up to the Second Coming of Christ… do they sleep and in an instant rise at the Second Coming, or do they go with the thief on the cross to Paradise, are they out of time completely, or are they, like the characters in Revelation 6, 20 and Hebrews 11 seem to be watching and observing us and shouting out for us.

I haven't had much cause to think about what we mean every time we say the Apostles Creed and recite:

I believe in the Holy Spirit, the holy catholic Church, the communion of saints, the forgiveness of sins…

What did the authors have in mind?

But imagine they are there today, cheering you on. Your great aunt Mabel who no-one else knew much about but you imagine has been received into heaven with treasures galore. The theologians, bishops, and ministers who in this life received abundant praise and may or may not have stored up treasures in heaven as well. The missionary martyrs. The ancient celts. The disciples of Jesus. What if they were shouting 'How Long O Lord' on your behalf? What if they could see a perspective you can't and were still cheering you on?

Wouldn't that be an encouragement as the Day approaches?

Wouldn't that spur you on?

I had reason recently to kneel at the cross of St Patrick in Downpatrick, and then at St Hilda and St Cuthbert's icon/tomb respectively in Durham Cathedral. Not to venerate the dead. Not to bypass the Lord Jesus Christ the only mediator and advocate but to enjoy the communion of saints. To remember that I (and my generation) are not on our own. To remember that bishops have faced far harder things than nailing their colours to the LLF mast. To remember echoes of history like Luther's 'Here I Stand, I Can Do No Other' or like Polycarp:

"Eighty and six years have I served Christ, nor has He ever done me any harm. How, then, could I blaspheme my King who saved Me? … I bless Thee for deigning me worthy of this day and this hour that I may be among Thy martyrs and drink the cup of my Lord Jesus Christ."

Dear friends, we 'charismatics' are a very young church, but our family likeness goes back down the centuries, past the apostles, and prophets to the patriarchs of faith.

We have much to learn and be inspired by, and perhaps even more friends close to hand than we first thought.

Don't look back in anger, but do remember the rock from which you were hewn. It will help you for today and for tomorrow.

Chapter Eight:
Here Come The Generals

Dear Friends,

This week I've had the chance to travel with one or two of the generals of the UK church to observe and learn from some of our partners around the Anglican world. One I was particularly delighted to travel with, as I have owed a huge amount to him ever since I heard him speak about 'how and why I can be filled with the Spirit' on VHS tape in 1996. This was a clear turning point in my life.

Awaiting us in Cairo were recognised generals from their own worlds - as Anglican Archbishops gathered for their Global South Fellowship of Anglicans (GSFA) meeting with invited observers attending.

You know the feeling as a kid at school when you wandered into the staff room?

Of course, I've been around just about long enough to know that some of the people who seem a lot in the world's eyes may not be so much in eternity, (and vice versa), but there was a humbling integrity in the room and my traveling companions that impressed me. It is not inevitable that you gain the whole (ecclesiastical) world and yet lose your very soul. Some manage to march forward on their knees.

Remembering Rowan

Ironically perhaps this reminded me of being in the room with Archbishop Rowan Williams as a young curate when he was doing what he did best. Living the cruciform life. Patterning himself on the way of Jesus. Putting others interests before himself. I remember acrimonious debates at Synod on the Global Communion, the Windsor Report, or similar, and his interventions at the end. Rarely to swing the debate to his personal position. Mainly to pray.

I found myself describing this to my spiritual director over zoom from my prayer shed as I prepared to travel. I was imagining Rowan as a pacifist General of church who would lay down his life for the sheep when his rod and his staff proved insufficient defensive weapons. After a heated debate Archbishop Rowan would ask us to rise. He would invoke a Spirit-fuelled silence that brought a depth and holiness into the room of majestic proportions, and led our troubled hearts to the still, still waters he had presumably helped cultivate in years of disciplined prayer and obedience and a million acts of laying down his own life and right to 'choose his own way to go'. He opened up a spiritual reality resonant of Jesus' beatitude: Blessed are the Peacemakers. A pacifist 'General' with an eirenic spirit we still need today. He let himself be crucified to hold the Lord's beloved church together.

Canterbury?

One of the debates in the Communion was until recently, if the office of Canterbury survives the current controversies, could another non-Englishman be appointed, and, more radically, could it be a Global South Archbishop who is chosen to lead the Anglican Communion? Just as an Argentinian outsider has shaken parts of the papacy, with what has seemed to many as a radical humility, could a South Sudanese, Chilean, Indian or Malaysian fill the international third of the role (leaving the Diocesan and National aspects to an English man or woman)? It is certainly a job that needs breaking into three, and there is good reason for us in England to want to receive such ministry on these shores as well. But that all seems desperately unlikely now.

At SOMA we talk about long distance birds, albatrosses, bringing back olive branches of hope from around the Anglican World to the UK. It's hope we sorely need in England. As we seem to be recessing into our age of senility, easily forgetting where we have come from, other parts of the Communion are coming of age as young and mature adults capable of leading a vibrant and spiritual church.

Cairo

It was a joy to travel with Nicky and Pippa Gumbel, who were both visiting Alpha International, and preaching at the Cathedral on the following Sunday as well as Nicky being an unofficial voice for the broad 'alliance' of parties 'compelled to resist the House of Bishops' as an observer at the GSFA meeting. It was humbling to hear their heart and passion for the church and there is at least one photo going around of me looking like a fan-boy around them. We were joined in the invited guests from the Church of England by John Dunnett, who I have known since doing ARROW on the CPAS leadership scheme and who now spends his time networking and encouraging the troops though the umbrella group

CEEC. Sitting between two such 'generals' in these meetings was an honour.

Six other observers included representatives from two mission partners, the remnant of 'orthodox bishops in The Episcopal Church (USA) a bishop with substantial experience in the DRC Congo from Australia who now has an international remit and two reps of the Anglican Church in Europe lead bishop who couldn't be there.

This broad range of observers perhaps represented the optimists, the realists and the pessimists when it came to direction of travel in the Church of England, with even the most optimistic passionately arguing that they should send a strong warning to the House of Bishops that it will have very serious consequences for the communion, and asking that the Primates align themselves with the Anglican Alliance and Orthodox in the Church of England and don't leave us if we can turn this around.

Nicky emphasised that he was speaking in his personal capacity, not on behalf of organisations associated with his name. But he was passionate about the name of Jesus being honoured. And this was his very personal story of resisting his friend of more than 40 years.

"I've ducked this issue for many years, but I got into it when I saw it was going to divide the Church of England and the Anglican Communion etc… I had to step in."

"I don't want to be part of any other body that doesn't include all of you here," he said, and, "If we stop it please don't throw us out, align yourselves with us who are orthodox still."

It was a plea for unity that stretched beyond formal unity at Provincial level, and felt like a 'here comes the general' moment (from the bit in the musical when George Washington arrives on the scene).

It was harrowing to hear even the most optimistic voice argue that he only had a plan A - to stop this - as anything else would be the death of the Church of England. The death wouldn't happen overnight, but it would set in from the day you change doctrine, and would ruin all the unity that had been worked so hard for. It was chronological snobbery, a racist worldview and Anglican arrogance – saying 24 bishops in Church of England are right and the Orthodox/Pentecostals/Catholics/and all of you are all wrong… it is "nonsense and we have to stop it."

That was the final impassioned speech of a long session, and combined with some factual updates the following day left a lasting impression on the Primates. The Primates were keen to hear from the observers, and the pleas clearly had an effect in the room with the chair reiterating the promise that the Anglican Communion will never leave the orthodox in England on their own.

And while the Primates heard the case that 'nothing had actually changed yet' after February at Synod and the assertion that 'until the prayers have been commended (in December 2023) nothing would have actually happened,' they were nevertheless largely nonplussed by the idea that it could be the General Synod holding Archbishops and Bishops back from changing doctrine.

For them 'as go the bishops, so goes the church'. It's the Bishops' job to defend doctrine, it should not be left to the laity or clergy to fight the battles their 'shepherds' are supposed to lay down their lives for. But they heard the legal fact that nothing yet has been decided despite press releases and conferences from the most senior clergy in England that had sowed confusion around the Communion.

No-one quite knows where this will land, and for those in the peripheries of churches where we have laid few foundations for understanding the counter-cultural worldview of 'dying to self' rather than 'affirming self' this will be a change of pace many are ill-equipped to cope with. It's one of the reasons it's helpful to hold up to ourselves the mirror of history and the mirror of our Global church partners. While none of us have the whole Truth - that title lies with Jesus alone - we get perspective when we listen to those who are ready and able to lay down their lives for him. We get to consider whether the Christianity we have been marketing is an adequate summary of his message at all.

Whilst it was good to travel with our UK 'Generals', there was a real sense that the Communion has now been reset to the Global South. A hundred or so years ago 90% of Anglicans were in England. Now you'd be generous to claim it was 25%, as you'd have to assume we have 20+million Anglicans, when 90% of them rarely attend church). The church has moved South. And the new generals have often lived through wars, religious persecution, threats to their lives, poverty and the like. They are unlikely to be as cowered into submission as elements in the Church of England seem to be.

'Take up your cross, deny yourself and follow Him', is their message. It is a costly call that takes you beyond the self-affirmation of 'he loves me just the way I am'. It takes you to a far more dramatic conclusion. 'He loved me while I was still his enemy, died for me, and calls me to sin no more. He calls me to die to my old way of life and be re-born into a new one. He calls me get to realise that to live is Christ and to die is gain. He calls me to a sanctification process where I am changed from glory unto glory'.

Whether that message can land in our 'mile wide and inch deep' Church of England and 'mile wide and inch deep' charismatic circles is another matter entirely. It's been a long time since we dug deep for the old, old wells of spiritual vitality that once drenched these islands in the Spirit. Is there any chance we can hear the cry of the new Global South 'Generals' and dig deep once more?

Chapter Nine:
You Will Receive Power

Dear friends,

"God is wanting to raise up apostles and prophets in the Anglican Church." These were the words of Revd Buli Wooley, my SOMA counterpart in South Africa, at the 2023 Anglicans Ablaze conference attended by many of their provincial bishops. It gave me a surge of hope as she described it. In and through the institutional mess of the Anglican Church God was looking to raise up people full of the Spirit's power, uncompromised in convictions, ready and willing to follow Him wherever it goes.

Leaving aside for a moment what 'apostles and prophets' may be in our context it is too all easy for people to get trapped before they can grow into their calling. Some years ago, I was contacted by a trusted intercessor who said she had a dream for me: In it I was strapped down in my basement in a dentist chair while two men in suits tried to operate on me. Fairly swiftly I checked this out with a prophetic dream interpreter from an older generation. The sense from this and other images in the dream was these were two different institutions trying to control me.

In an earlier chapter I talked about 'Hagars'. I talked about them as people who have been used by 'people of promise' (like Abraham and Sarah) to short-circuit vision. Michael Everitt wrote to say:

"I like your use of Hagar. It does presume that the 'others' are Abraham (people of promise). But often it is akin to Joseph. Joseph brings prophetic words and vision that so challenged the brothers that they seek to kill him, [but] then sell him into slavery."

But what men meant for harm, God used for good. The slave rose up, and preserved the nation.

Whether you have been thrown in a well, trapped in a chair or otherwise discarded, what God wants to raise up he will raise up. And he will transform you along the way.

If I were to define prophetic and apostolic at their simplest it would be people who can speak and act through God's power… I'm not talking about 'apostolic' as people who are a bit entrepreneurial, or prophetic as people who like saying challenging things to power. Nor am I talking about those who hold an office in the institutions, although all of these things may overlap. I'm talking about slaves to Christ, laying down their own lives, marked by God's empowering presence evidenced through miracles, signs and wonders and prepared to persevere and suffer for it (cf 2 Corinthians 12).

Now that would be quite an Anglican church.

An army of slaves

Some years ago, Pete Greig inadvertently launched a prayer movement with his vision of an army of slaves to the hurting and dying, an army of dangerously pure young weirdos and freaks who had given up on the game of minimum integrity, fasting essentials and who were free from materialism. They were willing to lay down their lives for a man on death row and pray like a dying man with groans beyond talking, with warrior cries, sulphuric tears and with great barrow loads of laughter!

Waiting. Watching. 24-7-365. Their DNA chooses JESUS. (He breathes out, they breathe in.) Their subconscious sings. They had a blood transfusion with Jesus. Their words make demons scream in shopping centres. Don't you hear them coming?

At a similar time, Martin Smith was inviting us to be history makers. We proclaimed that it is true today that cloudless skies will break, kings and queens will shake, dead men will rise and the blind will be set free as people stand with the fire of God, and the truth in hand. We announced that we'll see miracles, we'll see angels sing, we'll see broken hearts making history, and wrapped up the anthem with "Yes, it's true and I believe it. We're living for you."

By 2001 Pete Greig's poem was inspiring 100,000 underground churches in China, but Pete had to work this out in a very different context – in one of London's 'megachurches' in Kensington and then in a plush commuter town where average house prices are close on £600,000. He also had to work it out in the rough and tough of life he documents so well.

I guess the question is: Does this army of slaves survive affluenza? Does it keep marching when God is on mute?

Are there any history makers?

Is it true today?

I want to shout "Hell, Yes, it is true…" and see those demons shudder.

We're only 20-30 years on and it often takes God a lot longer to form people than that. It may be easier to descend into a delusional deconstructionism, but these (then) young men were onto something that won't go away. A Kingdom that is forcefully advancing.

Why power is needed and not (just) a dirty word

Luke's portrayal of Jesus is that he was conceived in power, baptised in power and ministered in power that amazed all around him. His disciples were not to do anything after his ascension until they too had been 'clothed in power from on high'.

In Acts the apostles 'receive power', minister in 'great power', and even deacons appointed to serve at tables can be described as 'full of grace and power'.

Peter describes how this power countered the power of the devil. "God anointed Jesus of Nazareth with the Holy Spirit and power, and how he went around doing good and healing all who were under the power of the devil, because God was with him." Acts 10:38

Paul's personal testimony to the Romans was that:

"I will not venture to speak of anything except what Christ has accomplished through me in leading the Gentiles to obey God by what I have said and done, by the power of signs and wonders, through the power of the Spirit of God. So from Jerusalem all the way around to Illyricum, I have fully proclaimed the gospel of Christ." (Romans 15:19)

And to the Corinthians: My message and my preaching were not with wise and persuasive words, but with a demonstration of the Spirit's power, so that your faith might not rest on human wisdom, but on God's power. (1 Cor 2:4-5). The kingdom of God is not a matter of talk but of power (1 Corinthians 4:20)

Crucially while this divine power enables us to demolish strongholds, arguments and pretentious that set themselves up against the knowledge of God, (2 Cor 10:3-5), Paul also says that the power at work in him/us is made perfect in human weakness so that there can be more of God and less of us. (2 Cor 12).

He warns Timothy about people who 'have a form of godliness but deny its power'. Presumably in the context the power he was talking about that power had to do with the power of a changed life as he has just given a litany of sins that will be seen in the last days including loving pleasure, loving themselves and loving money, but without having real love, forgiveness, gratitude or holiness. A true form of godliness should change all that, even though (as he goes on to say) everyone who wants to live a godly life in Christ Jesus will be persecuted.

Understandably, and tragically, almost everything to do with 'power' in the Christian church at the moment is under scrutiny. That's an obvious issue for a movement that was radically renewed in the 1980s by John Wimber's teaching on Power Healing, Power Evangelism and Power Points.

Human power is unavoidable.

Human power dynamics begin as soon as two people come together. Human power needs handling with great care. It can easily corrupt. If we reflect on all of life's relationships most of us have more power than we immediately realise. We'll return to how power needs to be handled next week, although a good adage from the world of safeguarding is:

> Hold power lightly | Use power wisely | Share power widely
>
> Jeanette Plumb

And it is easy for a movement to shift from seeking God's power to holding on to human power. As it gains momentum, money, and respect it has something to protect.

But what if Pete Greig and Martin Smith were right. What if God was looking for history making weirdos and freaks, whose goal isn't power, miracles, history making or revival, but slowly and gradually as the refiner's fire blazes whose goal becomes Jesus himself?

What if we feel like we've been locked away from this potential for years, stuck in an Egyptian jail with Joseph, a shepherd's hillside with Moses, back in Tarsus with Saul, watching and waiting with Anna and Simeon (or maybe even stuck in a dentist chair while institutions operate on us). Slowly discombobulating. Dying to self. Realising we can do nothing apart from Christ.

What if all this was in God's plan.

What if all this time God has been trying to teach us to be slaves in order to truly set us free.

What if the God who trains hands for war (Ps 144) is still raising up an army?

Just as the institutions start to crumble away, what if his plan is to once more raise up an order of people who are marked by the miraculous, who will suffer for His name, who are slaves of Christ?

What if our movement that began with 'Power' is supposed to still operate in that power, a power only to be safely yielded by those who know themselves to be truly weak?

Hear again the words of the dreamer… Let's not forget what we are here for.

Don't you hear them coming? Herald the weirdos! Summon the losers and the freaks. Here come the frightened and forgotten with fire in their eyes. They walk tall and trees applaud, skyscrapers bow, mountains are dwarfed by these children of another dimension.

Their prayers summon the hounds of heaven and invoke the ancient dream of Eden.

And this vision will be. It will come to pass; it will come easily; it will come soon. How do I know? Because this is the longing of creation itself, the groaning of the Spirit, the very dream of God. My tomorrow is his today.

My distant hope is his 3D. And my feeble, whispered, faithless prayer invokes a thunderous, resounding, bone-shaking great 'Amen!' from countless angels, from heroes of the faith, from Christ himself. And he is the original dreamer, the ultimate winner.

Guaranteed.

[The Vision: 24/7]

Chapter Ten:
Getting Out Of The Swamp

Dear friends,

Last week I spoke about a dream someone had had for me. Strapped in a dentist chair, hidden in a basement, being operated on by powerful suited men who I came to understand represented the institutional church and charismatic networks each trying to modify me for their own purposes. We looked briefly at the Joseph story, where he was thrown underground (twice), first by his natural family network and then by the institution he is serving when his words were not accepted. Today I want to broaden this more widely to gently offer a warning to brothers and sisters in the charismatic movement. It is the metaphor of standing in a swamp. It may be in a lush forest. It may be in beautiful surroundings, but that crusty surface we've been relying on can't hold us much longer, and for many, the reality is we are already sinking.

I'm drawing on our experiences in the Church of England for this, but am sure that there will be parallels wherever you have been relying on the world for promotion, position or prosperity. There can be little doubt that the Church of England is a worldly church, rebirthed in the reformation era out of one man's desire to commit adultery, and ladled with all the trappings of wealth and access to power that Jesus himself regularly warned could corrupt a soul.

It reminds me of a visitor to the Vatican who was apparently shown around the treasure-filled vaults and proudly told by a Cardinal: "No longer do we have to say 'silver and gold have I none'" [like St Peter to a cripple in the book of Acts]. To which the visitor (perhaps in a Scottish accent) re-joined: "Aye, but can you still say, 'In the name of Jesus of Nazareth, Rise up and Walk.'"

Two Dreams

I take the idea of the swamp from an intercessor at the large conference I attended this summer. I'd felt the need to get up early and pray after a challenge from a mentor over the previous couple of days. As I walked around the still quiet campsite I heard a voice call, 'Richard, I thought I'd see you here.' There was my friend and ministry colleague also out walking. She is a bit like Joseph in that she has a ministry of prophetic dreams and interpretation. As we carried on walking and praying, she described how she had been disturbed in the night by two dreams. One of a swamp and the other of a meat market. I later asked her to give a summary of the meaning of those dreams. The meat market was in part a warning against 'transactional spirituality' where you expect God to do things because you have shown up in a certain way and asked/demanded that he does it. I'll come back to that another time, not least as it begs lots of questions about who might be treated as the meat, but I want to focus this chapter on the swamp.

The swamp

The swamp was the ground that looks solid, until you step on it and find yourself up to your neck in swamp water. The foundation were wobbly – it looked alright on the surface, but underneath something was wrong. There's a bit in a Terry Pratchett book (youthful reading!) where the witches (don't groan) land in a swamp, thinking it's solid ground: "But even you couldn't tell it was water," said Magrat. "It looks so… so grassy."

To explore this image, I want to think of three reasons (perhaps there are many) whereby you might have ended up standing in a swamp when you thought you were on solid ground, before asking how a swamp might get formed in the first place when we think of ourselves a movement that embraces the 'River of Life'. These reasons resonate with Jesus' three warnings in the parable of the sower: "The worries of this life, the deceitfulness of wealth and the desire for other things." [Mk 4:19] all have the potential to choke the life right out of us.

1. The Emotional Handbrake Turn (Exit) Swamp

As we have explored in earlier chapters, charismatics have lived with unprecedented favour for a season in the institutional church. Whereas our forefathers, like John Collins, found themselves ostracised and pitied for their enthusiasms, a declining and desperate Church of England has slowly embraced a tame form of charismatic endeavour, mainly because it is the part of the church where the kids, youth and ordinands have tended to come from. This embrace has included institutional roles and institutional monies. The palace is the limit for today's charismatic Anglicans.

So, when HTB church leaders, New Wine church leaders, and older Renewal church leaders suddenly find themselves at odds with the institution it is an emotional handbrake turn. When 'we can trust Justin' becomes a 'he is not listening to me' in a few short months it's a sudden departure from easy street. You can stay on that easy street if you're prepared to bow the knee to the 'newspeak' that doctrine has not changed while doctrine has changed, but if you challenge that BAM! One minute you're running a successful church plant, the next minute a bishop is hauling your staff team into their office to 'talk about their jobs'. One minute you are interviewing for a diocesan role, the next minute you're being attacked in an orchestrated social media campaign. All of which may in fact be doing us a favour.

In 1 Corinthians 10:12 St Paul issues the memorable line: "Be careful when you think you are standing lest you fall".

When we've been standing on the edge of a swamp, sirened in by worries about life, the allure of Queen Anne's bounty and the desire for position and promotion, it's actually a gift to see the swamp for what it is. To take a step back and try to remember that the 'solid ground' is God's word – reserved as Jesus puts it for the one who "hears these words of mine and puts them into practice". [Mt 7:24] It is possible to amass power, influence and possibilities in this life and in the next life find you have been building very little. It may look 'so grassy' but if it's neither a 'green pasture' to be lead through nor a 'river of life' to revive the soul then why head into the swamp? It will slowly suffocate the spiritual life out of you. The worst of it is, you may not realise what it was until you sink.

2. History Maker? Swamps

There is a swamp in the John Bunyan classic: Pilgrim's Progress. He imagines the swamp represents despondency. A despondency that can stop you on your journey before you really start. He calls it the 'slough of despond.'

There is a despondency that seems to hit people on a journey out of charismatic experience and identity. It is a sense of despondency captured well by the proverb: 'Hope deferred makes the heart grow cold.'

As we explored in the last chapter there was a generation that grew up 'Delirious' in the UK. Our anthem, from Martin Smith's band Deliriou5 (where the final 's' was replaced with a very cool '5'), heralded the truth that when people pray, cloudless skies will break and Kings and Queens will shake. It announced that we'll see dead men rise and the blind set free. It proclaims that we'll see miracles, we'll see angels sing, we'll see broken hearts making history. And all of these statements are verifiable truths in a global and historical church. People have and do still receive all of these things. But…

But… and it is a huge BUT for many…

But… few of those who chanted the words 'I want to be a history maker' in the 1990s have lived to see anything like that reality in their personal, family, church or national contexts.

Few have seen God's power like that.

Few have seen God heal

Those closest to them

Let

Alone

Heal

A nation

Most have lived with tragedy. This world is full of sorrows.

In a Harry Potter era where a wand can fix most things temporal, the history makers have seemed like history observers. In a world that seems on a trajectory to out of control, we don't get to break cloudless skies at our every whim. And we don't get to heal all cancer, hurt, pain, childlessness, and sorrow.

(And we're no longer expecting revival either, because how long can we live in 'pre-revival days' anyway, when our friends and family are still not en masse entering the Kingdom).

We feel impotent, spiritually speaking.

Did we confuse signing up to being miracle makers with taking up our cross?

Did we sign up to be a history maker or a disciple of Christ?

Was the miracles/purpose what we really wanted in the first place?

And when we didn't get the gifts, (however age inappropriate they may have been for our underdeveloped spiritual persona), what do we do with the giver? Do we leave Him too? Probably easier not to leave Him per se, but definitely avoid His family, and then just meet with Him less often as He's always hanging out with them anyway and then maybe relegate him to an emergency contact on our smart phone which is more reliable at giving me a spiritual/emotional hit anyway as it meets my dopamine needs in a way Jesus just can't anymore.

We sink into the swamp.

3. 'Relationship with Jesus' Swamps

There's another way into despondency too. Another well cut path into the slough of despond. And it is a surprising one.

It's the (misunderstood) marketing of a 'relationship with Jesus'. A tempting diving board into the swamp.

The consistent invitation of the charismatic church has been to have a 'relationship with Jesus'.

It is good marketing, as if there is one thing that people long for more than a purpose, or power; it is the Bridget Jones mantra: 'to be loved just the way I am'.

The problem is that this relationship has been sold to a consumer generation as a satisfaction for their deepest needs.

But this is a 'swipe-left / swipe-right' generation, who have come to understand relationships in disposable terms.

If the relationship with Jesus fails to meet whatever I feel my deepest needs are, my instinct is to quickly desert Him.

If he is not numbing my pain, or incomprehensibly starts leading me in the valley of the shadow of death I shout out that this is not the 'desire of my heart' and stop delighting in him – if I ever did in the first place.

'My Jesus, my saviour' gets the boot as my surrogate boyfriend/lover/friend.

He failed to 'complete me' (as I understood 'complete').

So two years in, or at the 'seven year itch', or when the kids have grown up/got into church school and I'm not doing it for them anymore, I slowly and unthinkingly (or dramatically and decisively) find myself separate from him.

Jesus and his family become just another in a string of relationships that did not last the course. Another failure. Another way back into the swamp.

This is the tragic legacy of a church inviting a profoundly egalitarian generation to 'a relationship with Jesus' without explaining the parameters. A generation thinking we were entering a relationship with Jesus as equals/individuals. Aren't all relationships supposed to be like that? A generation not implicitly understand that He is the Master, the Lord, the one to be obeyed, the author and perfecter of our faith. A relationship that we easily forget is a corporate invitation to belong to the bride of Christ – the church – not a one to one for an individual. A relationship that we forget requires us to be 'born again' to enter. To be baptised into a new life, having died to an old one. To an ongoing commitment to 'put to death whatever remains of that old way of life'.

And this is an invitation into a relationship that can tragically removes us from remembering the first person of the Trinity. The Father. The Almighty. The Maker of Heaven and Earth who disciplines those he loves.

All in all, a very different proposition to asking 'would you like to have a relationship with the only man who will never let you down?'

There is a whole level of despondency that comes when you realise Jesus didn't come to earth to be your ideal lover or to satisfy your need for purpose.

How does the swamp form?

If you are a charismatic the chances are it is because you, your church, your movement or your family have had a good long swim in the spiritual 'river of life' at some point in your history.

You may still be splashing and swimming, going deeper into that river Ezekiel prophesied and Jesus fulfilled. The trees growing near you may be for the healing of the nations. You may be refreshed, revived and released in ministry by the Spirit's ministry. You may have an ongoing encounter with the Spirit of Holiness that envisions, enables, equips and energises you for evangelism.

Praise God if you are.

You've avoided the swamp.

But what happens when a river gets blocked, or spreads out widely in its final sedentary phases, or changes course over time and stops flowing into an area it once brought life and vitality to?

Quite often it becomes a swamp.

If the swamp is what happens when a life-giving river runs out of energy in a wide flat plain. It happens when the river runs aground and doesn't have anywhere to flow. It happens when the river has changed course. It happens when the river ceases to get rejuvenated by fresh rains.

The swamp is where we get stuck when conditions have changed, and we have not changed with it.

There are those in the swamp who really should know better.

In the swamp are those with 'too much to lose' to move on. They're part of the machine. They're making a monument out of what was once a movement. The river may no longer be flowing but they have invested too much in the status quo to move now. The river may have moved, but the town they built on its banks still sustains them.

They are often those who find themselves employed in the charismatic industry. They are pastors, songwriters, speakers, writers, and church workers. Or perhaps they are those who have simply given so much they can't turn back.

Some, if they're honest, had their 'hope deferred one' too many times years ago. But they still head up their institution/their church/their network.

So they keep going until retirement.

Or they've invested all their social capital in friendship groups in those circles.

So they keep on keeping on.

They sing 'find me in the river' but are up to their neck in the swamp.

If they are lucky, they are balanced, head out of water, on long hidden stepping stones – stones that were once key rocks in an earlier spiritual adventure.

But if they lose their step a swampy baptism can be fatal. A final self-indulgence upsets their footing. The despondency they had been standing in having finally given way to sin. And the murky mud cakes them in shame even when if they eventually stumble out and leave the site where the river once flowed and head off into the spiritual barren lands.

But while they're in the mire they'll still hawk the swamp as 'living water' to anyone who will listen. With the zeal of a used-car salesman they promise purpose, miracles and relationship with Jesus, but they know almost nothing of any of the above. When their sins finally catch them out their sales pitch is over. They lose everything… or perhaps worse still, they gain 'freedom' from selling something that they stopped believing in.

Dear reader, I hope you are not in the swamp, or if you've got a toe, a foot or a leg in you can quickly pull it out. You may need help to do so, and you may need to help a friend, a church, a network or a movement to do the same.

Of course, I am delighted that there are always those who have never believed these half-truths, those who have a mature reflection on disappointment, suffering and pain, those who have found miraculous events have punctuated their journey. Those who knew that Jesus was Lord because He told them.

But let justice flow like rivers. Let history makers awaken from slumber. Let those sold a relationship with Jesus be born again and know Him and His Father in all their glory as Lord, and Saviour as well as friend… Let those in the swamp see the prophets at the edges holding up signs saying 'Ichabod' ['the glory has departed'] and come to their senses. Let them hear the words of the faithful bible teachers reminding them of the pilgrimage they are to go on. Let them take the hands of the pastors who get a foot into the swamp with them to help them out again. Let them heed the evangelist's cry: 'repent and believe the good news'. Let them see where the apostles are building new paths to where the river is now flowing, paths of juice and transformation, paths that irrigate new deserts that need conquering.

The swamp is not our past and it is not our destination.

When we are stuck in it is time to move.

Chapter Eleven:
You See Dry Bones? I See An Army

In the last couple of chapters I want to bring us back to some of the core contributions we charismatics can bring to the church of God. Yes, we are a young church in the scheme of church history, but there's no reason to be a baby anymore. In Chapter Nine, 'You Will Receive Power', we looked at Pete Grieg's rousing vision. "You See Dry Bones?" he challenged. "Well, I See An Army." It's a vision that echoes the book of Ezekiel. But to get to the resurrected army of Ezekiel 37 we have to go through Ezekiel 34.

The meat market:

Ezekiel, the prophet sent to his own people, who needs a 'forehead of flint' to even talk to them, turns his fire in Chapter 34 on the spiritual leaders of his day. He accuses them of running a spiritual meat market.

The very people who are supposed to be feeding the sheep, preserving the sheep for the master, saving the sheep from danger have the sheep 'in their mouths'.

Ezekiel 34

The word of the Lord came to me: "Son of man, prophesy against the shepherds of Israel; prophesy and say to them: 'This is what the Sovereign Lord says: Woe to you shepherds of Israel who only take care of yourselves! Should not shepherds take care of the flock? You eat the curds, clothe yourselves with the wool and slaughter the choice animals, but you do not take care of the flock. You have not strengthened the weak or healed the sick or bound up the injured. You have not brought back the strays or searched for the lost. You have ruled them harshly and brutally. So they were scattered because there was no shepherd, and when they were scattered they became food for all the wild animals. My sheep wandered over all the mountains and on every high hill. They were scattered over the whole earth, and no one searched or looked for them.

"'Therefore, you shepherds, hear the word of the Lord: As surely as I live, declares the Sovereign Lord, because my flock lacks a shepherd and so has been plundered and has become food for all the wild animals, and because my shepherds did not search for my flock but cared for themselves rather than for my flock,   therefore, you shepherds, hear the word of the Lord: This is what the Sovereign Lord says: I am against the shepherds and will hold them accountable for my flock. I will remove them from tending the flock so that the shepherds can no longer feed themselves. I will rescue my flock from their mouths, and it will no longer be food for them."

Fast forward to New Testament times where Jesus the Good Shepherd still calls 'pastors' to help 'feed his sheep'. We're supposed to 'smell of the sheep' because we block their path to destruction when they need a rest or start to wander. We're supposed to 'smell of the sheep' as we would lay down our lives for them, imitating the Cross-bearer.

If there is lamb stew on our breath, or mint sauce on our table, we are in a whole heap of spiritual trouble.

It's easy to do.

Remember Eli's children who young Samuel replaced as prophets. They were feeding off the sacrifices received for Yahweh. That prophet lost his life because he wouldn't protect God's people from his own children's indulgent appetites.

Remember Gideon when he had that mighty victory after his half-right rally cry: "For the Lord and for Gideon"? He rightly turns down being King but can't hold back from the allure of wealth. £650,000+ of gold in today's prices is handed over to him as thanks for his victory. But it becomes a snare to him and his sons and by the end of the account he is remembered no more. He can't quite get over the idea that he is owed something for his victory. Maybe he said to himself, "I am doing this for my children"? "I'd fight these battles just for you Lord, but my children need xy and z in return."

Whether we have responsibility for 10, 50 or 100 of the Lord's precious sheep the basic questions Ezekiel makes us ask is:

"Are we letting his people become food for wild beasts or are we defending them?"

"Do we 'smell of the flock' or smell like we have been feasting on the flock?"

Table 6: Church size distribution summary, 2019 and 2022[f]

	5th percentile		25th percentile		median (middle) church		75th percentile		95th percentile		mean (average) church	
	2019	2022	2019	2022	2019	2022	2019	2022	2019	2022	2019	2022
Worshipping Community	9	8	21	19	45	37	95	80	248	220	77	67
All age average weekly attendance	3	2	13	10	34	25	78	58	190	144	58	44
Adult average weekly attendance	3	2	12	9	30	22.5	67	50.5	157	121	50	38
Child average weekly attendance	0	0	0	0	2.5	1.5	10	7	34	25.5	8.3	6.1
Adult Usual Sunday attendance	7	6	14	12	25	22	50	40	120	93	41	33
Child Usual Sunday attendance	0	0	0	0	2	1	6	5	25	20	6.1	4.7
Easter attendance	0	0	25	18	51	38	102	75	250	181	79	58
Christmas attendance	0	0	32	23	80	56	197	133	563	397	157	109
Baptisms and thanksgivings	0	0	1	1	3	3	8	7	23	22	6.2	5.7
Marriages and services of prayer & dedication	0	0	0	0	1	1	3	3	8	8	2.1	2.1
Funerals in churches, crematoria, & cemeteries	0	0	1	1	4	4	10	9	28	25	7.9	7.2

The reality is there are less and less reasons to get into pastoring in the UK if you want to 'eat the sheep'. While the rich list of wealthy pastors in the world may be enough to make us all squirm, and accounts like 'preachersnsneakers' showing how much preachers pay for their shoes feels like dark comedy we find out this week that 95% of congregations in the Church of England have less than 93 adults on an average Sunday. Add in a demographic time bomb to that (where you are ten times more likely to be 80 than 18 if you are in church) it kind of looks like you'd look elsewhere if you wanted to be rich or famous. And add in the instability in the denomination and that basic security of stipend, housing, and pension looks precarious at best.

The dry bones

Today's charismatic pastors in the UK are being sent out to a valley of dry bones armed mainly with a key question:

"Son of Man / Daughter of Eve… can these dry bones live?"

They are surrounded by a cacophony of confused voices who question the very question:

'Do these bones really need to live?'

'Surely God loves the bones just the way they are?'

'Who are you to judge that the bones need be anything but a calcium deposit on the ground?'

'God will do what he wants with them anyway, won't he?'

'Isn't it a bit arrogant to say that these bones are dead?'

'Why would God want to raise them from their rest?'

'Isn't the idea of an army a bit outdated anyway?'

'God loves them just the way they are so who are you to say anything?'

'Surely these dry bones will be just the way they are for all eternity?'

'Why would you think they need your help?'

But may we rebel against the spirit of the age and the confusion spirit gripping the church and join Ezekiel's simple answer: "You alone know, Lord…"

You alone know, Lord… so speak, your servant is listening.

And as we do that listening the spiritually attentive among us hear the next two responses. They come from the Good Shepherd and echo through the ages. Can you hear him say: "Prophesy"?

Firstly speak to the dry bones: "Dry Bones hear the Word of the Lord"

"And then speak to those winds of God: "Come, breath, from the four winds and breathe into these slain, that they may live."

Word and Spirit come together and REVIVE what has been picked into a carcass by those who should have prophesied long ago.

That is the gift the charismatic church is supposed to be to the whole body of Christ… not a luller of lullabies helping euthanise a church into a sleep that lasts forever. Not a builder of human empires that cannot be taken with us through the refiner's fire that we must pass on the route to eternity. Not a feeding on the sheep class of shepherds getting fat on lamb stew. Not 'hired hands shepherds' who are happy to take a stipend while a church and world heads to a hell that they don't know if they believe in. But a Word and Spirit movement that is marked by a reverent awe of God's powerful word and knows how to bring life to the slain through the breath of God.

So this guy comes up to me and says, "What's the vision? What's the big idea?"

I open my mouth and words come out like this…

The Vision?

The vision is JESUS – obsessively, dangerously, undeniably Jesus.

The vision is an army of young people.

You see bones? I see an army.

And the army is discipl(in)ed. Young people who beat their bodies into submission.

Every soldier would take a bullet for his comrade at arms. The tattoo on their back boasts,

"for me to live is Christ and to die is gain".

Sacrifice fuels the fire of victory in their upward eyes. Winners. Martyrs. Who can stop them? Can hormones hold them back? Can failure succeed? Can fear scare them or death kill them?

And the generation prays like a dying man with groans beyond talking, with warrior cries, sulphuric tears and with great barrow loads of laughter!

Waiting. Watching. 24-7-365.

(24/7 Prayer)

I have a pastor friend in a well-known charismatic network whose church has attracted incomers from both charismatic and conservative churches. The conservatives are great, he says, as they have been so well taught that they sign up for a standing order to tithe to the church within the first three weeks. They're serious people who know there is a serious task that needs doing. They want to get involved. The charismatics he is naturally fond of frustrate as they often just want to know if the church feels good and float around the edges for a while wondering if they will get their spiritual high. But the ones who have really impressed him are those converted in a church that faithfully preached the word, and ministered in the power of the Spirit in order to reach the lost (not give a therapeutic high). These have integrated seriousness and joy unspeakable in a wonderful way. The tragedy was that they were converted all the way back in the early 1980s under the ministry of John Collins, the HTB vicar who could say 'all my theology is John Stott's' and who looked to John Wesley and George Whitefield for his inspiration.

That was the era when John Wimber could say 'we have an army'. Ten years later he was saying 'we have an audience'.

Dear charismatics: Our contribution to the church is to prophesy in order to raise up an army – not an audience.

But we need to remember the first prophecy is 'hear the word of the Lord'. It's a mighty word to sound out. It's a powerful word that brings dry bones back together into an army ready for the Spirit to move. While you're offering a wafer of positive platitudes based on prooftexts plucked from prophets who would have made you quake if you met them, you'll never offer the bread of life. We're supposed to be the people who make people turn to Scripture on their knees, who memorise the word, eat the word, and use it like a mighty sword (i.e., carefully).

Only then do we get to prophesy to the four winds to come and bring life. Until the word has brought the bones back together the wind would just scatter them further apart.

Can you hear the roar of heaven? Prophesy… prophesy. Today! There's an army to be called back together in every parish. It's time to offer bread of life and see who the Lord brings to feast with you.

There's an army that wants rising up, but it's waiting to hear from you.

Chapter Twelve:
Strength And Suffering

Dear friends

I was sitting at the start of last week in a prayer meeting of Anglican leaders praying for London. Prayers were orchestrated by leaders from the 'famous three': HTB, St Helen's Bishopsgate, and All Souls Langham Place, as well as by leaders from smaller churches in New Wine, Re:New and other networks. Evangelical leaders from across the streams, united as one river. A river bubbling in prayer as dozens of voices around the room led small groups in prayer, reminding me of student days. We prayed for an hour and a half, and I couldn't move from my seat for a little while afterwards. I just wanted to sit there and soak it in and pray some more.

I am rubbish at praying on my own, but put me in a room with others who want to pray and I take flight. I can't believe how easy it is or how impactful it becomes. I come away wondering why I don't do this all the time. It's partly muscle memory when I pray in those settings, and for that I have to thank my younger self who learnt more before he was ordained than he had since then. I learnt two things about prayer as a young Christian: The power of prayer and the need to practice.

The practice was simply that I had a year, aged 18, where I got up three mornings a week to pray with two people better than me at it, I learnt to pray to the beat of his Spirit, I fasted regularly (and sometimes stupidly) and prayed wherever I would go. I had a season at university where I was in charge of running 20+ weekly prayer groups for the world and I would visit as many as I could, and found praying for people you'd never met, and had no direct personal interest in, from the global church and 'unreached people groups' was a real accelerator in prayer life. I went to church prayer meetings before the services back home, at evening events, on Saturday mornings and caught as much as I could from those around me. I read great books on prayer, and hung the verse that begins 'If my people will humble themselves and pray' on my bedroom door. Crazy and intense as I may have seemed it scares me to remember the heights from which I have fallen sometimes to be honest…. Would my younger self have any truck with me now?

The Strength to Pray

In recent years, the thing that has helped me more than anything has been the realisation that prayer is best understood as a partnership activity with the Holy Spirit. A favourite prayer, drawn out of Romans 8, is to ask the Father (as almost all prayers in the NT are addressed to him):

> Dear Abba in Heaven, please would your gracious Holy Spirit who has already sealed my life and is here with us as we gather in Jesus' name, come and pray in us, with us, for us and through us now, in the name of Jesus, Amen?

The shorthand is: 'Holy Spirit, (please) come', but as with GCSE maths exams it's important to show our working, or we can drift into thinking the Holy Spirit is a force we somehow control.

As Arthur Wallis has shown in an exceptional book, the Holy Spirit helps us in our weakness…we provide the weakness, he provides the power… that's why (and when) prayer meetings can go on all night and fasting can prevail beyond natural levels. Dear friends, don't make the mistake of engaging in prayer as anything less than a supernatural activity that needs the wind of the Spirit to help you take flight. It's so foolish to do it on your own when your promised helper is Divine.

I was so moved by Wallis' book I wrote some summaries of each chapter for New Wine Online. Here is the key introduction:

The Spirit helps us in our weakness… Rom 8:26,27

The one place in the Bible that teaches us how the Spirit works as an intercessor is Romans 8. We learn that 1) he helps us in our weakness; 2) we do not know how to pray as we ought to; 3) the Spirit Himself intercedes for us; 4) He prays with groans too deep for words; 5) God knows the mind of the Spirit and searches our hearts; 6) The Spirit intercedes in accord with the will of God.

A few verses later (34) we also learn that Jesus intercedes for us. This is a distinct not duplicated ministry. This is crucial to understand.

Christ's intercession is apart from us at God's right hand (1 Jn 2:1), the Spirit's is within our hearts (Rom 8:27). Whether we are hot or cold, spiritual or carnal we cannot stop that intercession of Jesus. It is not affected by our ups and downs… what an encouragement to know that he has inscribed our names on His prayer list for all time.

But the intercession of the Spirit is very different.

It is a solemn fact that we can facilitate or frustrate the Spirit's intercession in us, by our co-operation or lack of it. Though Christ does not require us for His intercession the Holy Spirit most assuredly does for His. Here we can no longer be spectators. We must be participants. Christ prays for us in the sense that he makes us the object of His intercession, the Spirit prays in the sense that He makes us the vehicle of His intercession. He prays on our behalf by enabling us to pray, helping us in our weakness, who do not know how to pray as we ought.

The Spirit bears witness with our spirit… Rom 8:16

It is the Spirit who enables us to cry 'Abba Father' (Rom 8:15,16).. we do the crying but the Spirit inspires the cry. At Pentecost the disciples began to speak in tongues 'as the Spirit gave them utterance'…

The divine Spirit and the human spirit become joint witnesses by the cry that comes from within us… He needs us to accomplish His intercessory ministry, and we certainly need Him. He wants to be free to think though our minds, feel through our hearts, speak through our lips, and even weep through our eyes and groan through our spirits. When a believer is at the disposal of the Holy Spirit praying in the Spirit will become a reality.

Suffering

You'll have noticed that this power from the Spirit is given to us in our weakness.

Few of God's saints and fire starters have not been touched by pain. Like many others I have watched the 'Jesus Revolution' film recently about the 1970s Jesus People spiritual awakening among hippies. It is inspirational to watch thousands of baptisms in the sea at Pirates Cove and see an angle on how God opened hearts in that era.

But dig just a little deeper and you'll find that the inspirational and flawed character at the heart of it all was raped by a 17-year-old babysitter as an 8-year-old child just two weeks after being born again. Lonnie Frisbee (played by Jonathan Roumie who also plays Jesus in 'The Chosen') had also been brought up by a violent alcoholic dad and then later by a stepdad who hated him as his father had run off with that man's first wife. Yet some wounds run very deep in all of us. Some of those wounds he probably never fully recovered from. Indeed, he was expelled from and edited out of both the Jesus Movement and Vineyard stories after lapsing into cocktails of troubles and difficulties including a promiscuous homosexual lifestyle. He eventually died of AIDS. And yet in his ongoing brokenness he was still used to spark both the Jesus Revolution in the 1970s and to help Wimber kickstart the Vineyard movement in the 1980s.

It is no surprise that many people have turned to the charismatic movement for therapy. There is a lot of pain that needs processing.

It is no surprise that just a year after Frisbee died of AIDS his generation were still looking for an experience of the Father's love. Hence the impact of the Toronto Blessing on so many people. There are a lot of spiritual orphans out there. Boarding school survivors, bullied kids, kids with fathers who are 'absent, apathetic, addicted, achievement driven, authoritarian, abdicating or abusive fathers' (to use Mark Stibbe's categories. Stibbe's book *I am Your Father: What every heart needs to know* remains incredibly helpful, and although he was yet another minister who carried his own painful scars into a ministerial car crash, he too has now told the story of his early pain that contributed to the later wreckage).

When these pains are surrendered to God, they often become the 'cracks that let the light in'. When we try and self-medicate them away, they can destroy not just us, but those around us.

It's one of the reasons Dallas Willard started working with young leaders, trying to get them to process the dark side of their leadership style and personality and experience before it was too late. He dressed this up in a leadership course that has impacted many, but found that it was very hard to reach people later on in life if they hadn't processed at least some of that brokenness before they reached 40.

Some wounds don't heal easily.

But we charismatics have a contribution to the church here. We have a power from the Spirit, it is true. We have experience of seeing the Kingdom break in here and now, often in extraordinary ways. Cloudless skies do break. But we also know something of sharing in Christ's pain, that St Paul often alludes to.

Broadly speaking charismatics are often the 'feelers' in the church. It's not universally true but if you go to a town with a range of student churches if's often the case that you could pick what church you reckon a new student will end up at based on their personality profile. Some just like it straight, hard hitting and factual. Others like to be teased intellectually and get to think great thoughts. Many like to be embraced in a warm community bubble. Others want to feel that it is real.

To sit through 30 minutes of guitar-based ballads playing the same lyrics on repeat and starring into space with 'arms high and hearts abandoned' takes a certain sort of personality.

Sometimes it is thinkers who have found they connect to God best through another angle, bypassing their brain.

Often times it is deep feelers like the pop artist and lyricist Robbie Williams who sang:

> I just wanna feel real love | And life ever after | There's a hole in my soul | You can see it in my face | It's a real big place.
>
> [Feel, Robbie Williams, Guy Chambers]

But the pathos and the pain are an invitation to come to God, to share in Christ's pain for the world, to intercede and pray in the coming Kingdom. You almost need the pathos to carry the power. A love/compassion for the lost and broken to bring the health and healing. An inner brokenness to know that this treasure is not from us, but from Him, to carry around your jar of clay.

The enemy of turning pathos into prayer is distraction. Neil Postman wrote back in the 1980s about 'amusing ourselves to death' when we just had 4 channel television. Now we have dopamine anaesthetics in our pockets and tap the screens of our mobile phones to get a hit thousands of times a day. We self-medicate on social media, on games, on screens, on anything that distracts us from the pain, tedium, boredom, difficulties which are all supposed to be signposts to prayer for a people who know that the Kingdom they have experienced is still breaking in and forceful people are supposed to lay hold of it and bring its power to heal the planet and its people in the here and now. The pain, as CS Lewis said, is a megaphone – not just that we need God, but that He needs us (or at the very least wants us) to pray, pray, pray until something happens.

The pathos is the way into prayer.

If we inoculate from pathos, there is no prayer.

Because the Spirit is waiting to help us in our weakness. Our strength is seen where we are weak.

A final word

Charismatics had never felt so strong in the Church of England until a year or two ago. Now, those who are going to hold the line on biblical teaching on human sexuality have a choice. Behave as though we are strong and throw our weight around, or remember we are weak and use this season as a time to 'go into the desert', find our (new/alternative) spiritual overseers – our 'Abbas' and work on some of our own 'stuff' as we do so.

I've written about a 'Jacob and Rebekah' moment from my reflections of being at General Synod. It feels to me like a time pregnant with opportunity to re-find the way of the cross and walk the ancient paths. I hope we can choose the way of the cross once again and find our God in the desert teaching us the way of strength through suffering, and how he can work through weakness. As seen above when we forget our weakness and cling on to power it can derail us completely.

I'd rather be weak and filled with the Spirit.

At the end of the day: What profit it us if we gain the whole world, but lose our very soul.

Epilogue:
To The Desert

I am writing at a time of crisis in the Church of England where two tribes have gone to war, and where the flaws in all parts of the church have been badly exposed.

What happens when two brothers have deceived, tricked and let down their parents so much that they cannot stay under one roof? In the book of Genesis Mother Rebekah sends one of her sons off into the wilderness, thus protecting both the deceiver and the impetuous son. They both still bear the family name: 'Ben Isaac, Ben Abraham'. When they finally come back together, they somehow avoid killing each other, despite a bit of a face-off. Along the way they each mature, flourish, reflect, repent and wrestle.

I wonder if some wilderness wanderings would do us all some good – especially if we want a chance at staying as one Anglican family in the end… Ben Cranmer, Ben Augustine et al…

So what might a wandering off look like – for whichever 'son' should be sent out of the family camp for a time?

I wonder if the wander might be an ancient walk? A humble, penitent pilgrim walk that acknowledges our part in failing to pass on the faith once delivered and humbly heads to lay our heads on Bethel's stone, to gaze at the stairway to heaven who is the Son of Man (John 1), do the hard yards of learning to care for the flocks again, even in adverse circumstances, and finally wrestle with God until we gain our new name, new identity and learn how to minister in weakness not in strength.

Into the desert like ancestors of old.

The place where religious orders form.

A place where an army of 'Abba's and 'Abbesses' building a spiritual monastery of faith that will learn to move in word and spirit once more and go on missions up and down the land.

Such ancient orders had overseers who had jurisdictions apart from the episcopy. Abbots and Abbesses of remarkable faith, love, vision and holiness who called others to a rule of faith, sacrifice and obedience around them. People you could catch a vision from, catch a calling from, catch a gifting from.

Imagine a new reality: One where each person who wanted it could opt into a 'religious order' with an overseer who knew them by name, visited their churches, spoke into their lives, provided prophetic and pastoral feedback and accountability and called them upwards to a better future.

From this very month, 'Abbas' could emerge who already have an overseeing ministry distinct from the bishops. Abbots and Abbesses who provide the sort of overseeing that most people are crying out for anyway. All around the Church of England these men and women exist. They've often been overlooked for institutional roles, but naturally gather many around them. Several of them have spoken from the house of clergy here in Synod. Some may even be lay, and there may be retired or serving bishops who see this as a closer approximation to their real calling than the administrative function that can occupy much of the House and College of Bishops' times.

Friends, is this a time for a revolution…?

To establish a new form of spiritual abbey that can bring genuine life to this nation, and do the hard work of working on our own multiple failings while we are there.

As a religious order in the Anglican Communion / Church of England there will be things its novitiates (exploring belonging), oblates (lay members) and fully signed up members can and cannot be asked to do, determined by its rule of life.

It may be that this becomes the lifeboat built within a sinking ship. It might be that it does not fly at all. But for those who want the family to stay together it may well be the least tragic way of providing space to stay together that has yet been placed on the table, and it might even be the source of a whole new life and energy that ultimately comes back home as Jacob did and enables the family name to carry on and ensure the heritage of Abraham continued.

Printed in Great Britain
by Amazon

THE SEAL OF SIR RHYS AP THOMAS, from a replica in the Carmarthen Museum. The original seal was used on a letter written by Sir Rhys at Carmarthen in 1494. (*Transactions of the Carmarthen Antiquarian Society*, Vol. 26 (1936), facing p.15.)

THE STANDARD OF SIR RHYS AP THOMAS comprising the Cross of St. George; a black raven on a green mount, sprinkled with seven smaller ravens. The background of the standard is white. (College of Arms MS I.2. p.52)

Sir Rhys's quarterly coat of arms which appears above the standards, right, consists of Quarters 1 and 4, Argent, a chevron sable between three ravens sable; Quarters 2 and 3, Argent, on a cross sable, five crescents or, in the dexter canton a spear-head gules.

Quarters 1 and 4 are for Sir Rhys's family; Quarters 2 and 3 are for Janet, daughter of Gruffydd ap Llywelyn Foethus of Llangathen, a great-grandmother of Sir Rhys ap Thomas. (S. R. Meyrick (Ed.), *Heraldic Visitations of Lewis Dwnn*, Vol. 1. p. 210.)

SIR RHYS AP THOMAS

David Rees

First Impression—1992

© David Rees

ISBN 0 86383 744 1

This volume is published with the support of the Welsh Arts Council

Printed by:
J. D. Lewis & Sons Ltd., Gomer Press, Llandysul, Dyfed, Wales.

For Frances Oliver

By the same author

Korea: The Limited War
The Age of Containment
Harry Dexter White
Red Star Over Prague (Co-author)
The Korean War: History and Tactics (Consultant Editor and
    Contributor)
The Soviet Seizure of the Kuriles
A Short History of Modern Korea
Peaceful Coexistence: A Study in Soviet Doctrine
Rhys Davies ('Writers of Wales' series)
A Gower Anthology (Editor)
The Son of Prophecy: Henry Tudor's Road to Bosworth

CONTENTS

PREFACE

Sir Rhys ap Thomas (1449-1525) is best known for the part he played as Henry Tudor's chief Welsh ally at Bosworth Field (22 August 1485). This was an event of great importance in the history of both Wales and England and over a century later Shakespeare wrote in *Richard III* that amongst those who rallied to Henry, Earl of Richmond was 'Rice ap Thomas with a valiant crew'. When he died in 1525, laden with honour, Sir Rhys ap Thomas, K.G., Justice and Chamberlain of South Wales, had long been the most powerful Welshman of his era.

Sir Rhys played many roles. He was the greatest of the native Welsh magnates and virtually acted as deputy to the first two Tudor kings in West Wales. These monarchs were men whose trust was not easily won. Moreover Sir Rhys was the leading bardic patron of his day holding court at Abermarlais, Newton, Carew and other centres. Through his father Sir Rhys claimed descent from Urien Rheged of north Britain and on his mother's side he was certainly descended from the Welsh kings and princes. The poets regarded Sir Rhys with special favour praising him for his descent from the old British line and for his relationship to the Tudor kings who sprang from the same stock. He was of course quite rightly regarded as a great warrior.

This book thus attempts to tell the story of Sir Rhys with particular reference to his family and its origins, to his role in the Bosworth campaign, and to the part played later both as a Crown servant and as a bardic patron. We will finally assess the extent to which Sir Rhys's career preaged the great changes in Welsh government made under Henry VIII a decade or so after Sir Rhys's death in 1525. As a result of these changes modern Wales begins to take shape and thus Sir Rhys's career will surely remain a subject for continuing study.

I have indicated the scholars to whom I am most indebted by listing their works in the Bibliography. I am particularly grateful to Emeritus Professor Glanmor Williams who read the draft manuscript of this book and made a number of valuable suggestions. The late Dr E. D. Jones and Dr Eurwen Price helped me greatly with their translations of the Welsh poetic texts.

My thanks for assistance to Captain Denis Glover of the Pembrokeshire Museum, Haverfordwest, to Mr Roscoe Howells of the Pembrokeshire Historical Society, and to Mr Terrence James FSA of the Royal Commission on Ancient and Historical Monuments in Wales.

I am grateful for the ready help of the National Library of Wales and the Carmarthen Reference Library.

Grateful acknowledgement is made to the Carmarthenshire Antiquarian Society for permission to reproduce the drawing of Sir Rhys ap Thomas's seal and the picture of the Derwydd bedstead; to the College of Arms for the illustration of the Standard of Sir Rhys ap Thomas; to the Dyfed Archaeological Trust for the photographs of Sir Rhys's tomb and the Derwydd bedstead; to Mr John Lewis for the photograph of Neuadd house; to the Royal Commission on Ancient and Historical Monuments in Wales for the photographs of Weobley Castle and Sir Rhys's tomb-effigy; and to the Alan Shepherd studio for the photograph of Carew Castle.

David Rees

List of Illustrations

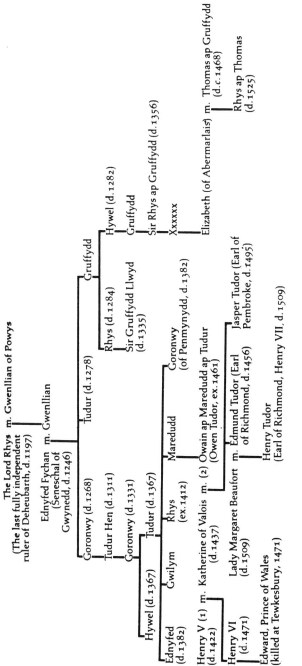

The Relationship between Sir Rhys ap Thomas and the Tudors

Chapter I
Family Background: The Landed Magnate

The roots of Sir Rhys ap Thomas's family lay far in the past of West Wales; the very antiquity and genealogical significance of the family had an important bearing on the events of Sir Rhys's life.

The Elizabethan genealogist Lewis Dwnn, who was a Deputy Herald at the College of Arms and a reliable antiquary, considered that Sir Rhys's family in the male line was descended from Goronwy ab Einion, once Lord of Iscennen and Kidwelly in Ystrad Tywi. This area later became part of Carmarthenshire. Dwnn recorded that the family claimed to trace its descent from Urien, a sixth-century King of Rheged, a region which corresponds to the modern Strathclyde and Galloway.

The Blood of the Raven

Urien Rheged's son, Owain, was reputed to have a bodyguard of fierce ravens. Hence the family motto of *Duw Gatwo'r Brain* ('May God Keep the Ravens') and its famous armorial bearings of three black ravens, expressed in heraldic terms as *argent, between a chevron sable, three ravens sable.* In the fifteenth century poets referred to the family as *Gwaed y Frân* ('The Blood of the Raven') and thus Rhys ap Thomas was often known quite simply as the Raven.

By the early fourteenth century when the family begins to appear in record evidence we find Elidir ap Rhys living at Crug near the banks of Nantrhibo, 'the bewitching stream', a site which survives to the present day as a smallholding on the outskirts of Llandeilo. According to Lewis Dwnn, Elidir's son was also named Elidir; his pilgrimage to Jerusalem brought him the title of Knight of

1

An armorial tile from Carew Church, Pembrokeshire, bearing a version of the arms of Sir Rhys ap Thomas. A number of these tiles were probably brought to the church from Carew Castle. (W. G. Spurrell, *The History of Carew*, 1922, facing p. 81.)

the Holy Sepulchre. Sir Elidir Ddu, or the Black Knight of the Holy Sepulchre as he was now sometimes known, married Elsbeth, a descendant of the Breconshire chieftain Moreiddig Warwyn, so giving the family an added status.

Again according to Lewis Dwnn, Sir Elidir Ddu was the first of his line to assume the family names of FitzUrien. This was an acquisition which, as we shall later in our story, was to prove literally fatal to the grandson of Sir Rhys ap Thomas.

Sir Elidir's son and heir was Philip, and he in turn was succeeded by his son Nicholas towards the end of the fourteenth century. He, too, lived at Crug which was described by an Elizabethan antiquary as 'a simple howse in the parish of Llandeilo'.

Nicholas was to marry Janet, a grand-daughter of Llywelyn Foethus ('the Luxurious'), a local, renowned magnate from the Llangathen area. The match was attended by unfortunate circumstances for Nicholas was wounded on his wedding day by a kinsman and soon died, but not before a posthumous son was conceived. That son, known as 'mab y dyn marw', the son of the dead man, was Gruffydd ap Nicholas. He was to become the leading

2

figure in West Wales in the mid fifteenth century, the founder of the House of Dinefwr, and the grandfather of Rhys ap Thomas.

Gruffydd ap Nicholas

Gruffydd ap Nicholas (c. 1400-c. 1460) was a man who displayed great capabilities and also great ruthlessness during his long and eventful career. According to a seventeenth-century family history, 'The Life of Rhys ap Thomas', Gruffydd was 'infinitely subtile and craftie, ambitiouse beyond measure, of a busie stirring braine'. What seems clear is that Gruffydd seized decisively the opportunities offered by a faltering English government in Wales in the aftermath of Owain Glyn Dŵr's rebellion (1400-1415) to acquire both public offices and private estates.

After holding minor offices in the Duchy of Lancaster Lordship of Kidwelly and in Carmarthenshire, Gruffydd was appointed sheriff of that royal county in 1426. By 1437 he began to act as Deputy Justice in Carmarthen, so acquiring the effective power of the highest royal official in the Principality of South Wales. The ever-growing weakness and insolvency of the Crown under Henry VI, and the common practice of appointing Welsh deputies to high English (but absentee) officials now meant that effective regional authority in West Wales passed to Gruffydd and his sons, John, Owain and Thomas, for a period of at least twenty years.

By the mid-1450s, Gruffydd and his affinity held the five strategic castles of the region; Carmarthen, Cardigan, Aberystwyth, Kidwelly and Carreg Cennen. In addition, in 1449, the Duke of York had transferred the Lordship of Narberth to Gruffydd and the Bishop of St. David's; to the end of his life Gruffydd considered himself Lord of Narberth. Gruffydd also held the Crown lordship of Emlyn; in the laconic words of D. L. Evans we learn that Thomas Hopton, who formally held the lordship after 1446, was quite unable to hand over his acquisition to his son Walter. For Thomas Hopton

> had been dispossessed forcibly by Gruffydd ap Nicholas and fear of the redoubtable Welshman kept Walter away from his patrimony. Gruffydd maintained his hold on the castle and the Lordship of Emlyn and they passed in time to his grandson Rhys ap Thomas in whose time the castle was restored.[1]

During 1439-40 Gruffydd ap Nicholas took a long lease of the royal lordship or demesnes of Dinefwr. The Lordship was adjacent to Crug and was a most important acquisition. On the site of the 'new town' of Dinefwr which lay slightly to the north of the medieval castle and its 'old town' Gruffydd built a hall (or *neuadd*) called Newton (Drenewydd). This manor house became his home and also a centre of bardic activities. Gruffydd ap Nicholas was a generous patron and presided over the great eisteddfod held in Carmarthen in about 1453. This was less an eisteddfod in the modern sense than a competitive meeting of bards which lay down new metric rules for the influential bardic fraternity.

The bards in turn held Gruffydd in high regard and in a famous ode Lewis Glyn Cothi hailed him as 'a chieftain from Urien' and 'the eagle of Carmarthen'. The poet believed that if King Arthur returned to West Wales then he would be calling for Gruffydd's help:

> Be byw'n Neheubarth, Arthur,
> Fal y bu a'r llu llawer
> Ef a alwai a'i filwyr
> Am blaid mab i Elidir . . .[2]

> ('Were Arthur living in Deheubarth today
> As he was with his numerous host
> He and his soldiers would be calling
> For support to the sons of Elidir . . .')

[1] J. E. Lloyd (Ed.), *A History of Carmarthenshire*, Vol. 1, 1935, p.240.
[2] E. D. Jones (Ed.), *Lewes Glyn Cothi (Detholiad)*, 1984, p.8.

4

Gruffydd was married three times. His first wife was Mabel, daughter of Maredudd ap Henry Dwnn of Kidwelly, his second marriage was to Margaret, the third daughter of Sir Thomas Perrot, and his third wife was Jane, daughter of Jenkin ap Rhys of Gilfach Wen near Llandysul.

From these marriages there were three surviving sons. John joined his father in leasing the Dinefwr lands in 1439-40, but little more is known of him. Owain was the heir of Cwrt Bryn-y-Beirdd near Carreg Cennen Castle and the companion in hiding of Lewis Glyn Cothi, possibly after the battle of Mortimer's Cross in 1461. (Lewis later addressed a *cywydd* to Owain.) It was through Gruffydd ap Nicholas's third son Thomas that 'the Blood of the Raven' passed to Rhys ap Thomas.

Thomas had acted as his father's agent in Cardiganshire in the 1440s eliminating opposition to the family's interests. He became Deputy Sheriff of that royal county as well as Escheator, and he had also held the post of Deputy Constable of Aberystwyth Castle. By 1455 Thomas, following his father's footsteps, was Deputy Justice of the Principality of South Wales, exercising his authority from Carmarthen Castle. Here was yet another example of what one historian of medieval Wales, Ralph A. Griffiths, has called 'government by deputy'.

Thomas ap Gruffydd had married Elizabeth of Abermarlais, daughter and heiress of the landowner and Crown servant, Sir John Gruffydd. This was a most advantageous alliance, for while Sir John's chief landed interests were in England, he also owned a number of estates in Carmarthenshire and Cardiganshire. These lands included the manor of Llansadwrn with its headquarters at Abermarlais and other properties at Llanrhystud, Llangybi, and Betws Bledrws in Cardiganshire. Most of these Welsh estates now became the portion of Elizabeth on her marriage to Thomas ap Gruffydd which took place at some time before 1446.

From this marriage there were six sons; Morgan, David, Rhys, Harry, Jenkin and John. The third son, Rhys ap Thomas was born in 1449.

They were not only landed assets which Elizabeth of Abermarlais brought to the family of Thomas ap Gruffydd ap Nicholas. Sir John Gruffydd was the direct descendant of Ednyfed Fychan (d.1246), the famous Seneschal (or Steward) of Gwynedd under Llywelyn the Great in the thirteenth century, and his wife Gwenllian, daughter of the Lord Rhys (d.1197). Like the other children of Thomas and Elizabeth, Rhys ap Thomas was thus descended from the royal rulers of Deheubarth who traced their lineage back to Rhodri the Great and Cadwaladr the Blessed.

Some of these properties in Elizabeth's marriage portion represented gifts which had been made by the princes of Gwynedd to Ednyfed the Seneschal. In this category came the Cardiganshire estate at Llanrhystud. But Llansadwrn itself with Abermarlais, which was later to be uniquely associated with Rhys ap Thomas, was probably a marriage gift made by Rhys Grug (d.1234), Lord of Dinefwr, to his sister Gwenllian, wife of the Seneschal.

Moreover, in a genealogical link that was to assume some importance in Rhys ap Thomas's career, both Rhys and Henry Tudor were descended from the marriage of Ednyfed Fychan and Gwenllian. The details are important in explaining a relationship that was well known to Rhys's contemporaries and formed a central part of his fame and influence, especially to the poets.

The Descendants of Ednyfed

Ednyfed the Seneschal and his wife Gwenllian had at least six sons. Of these the most famous were Goronwy, Gruffydd and Tudur. Both Goronwy (d.1268) and Tudur (d.1278) followed their father into the service of Gwynedd and acted successively as Stewards to Llywelyn ap Gruffydd (Llywelyn the Last, d.1282). By the time of the Edwardian conquest of Wales in 1282-83 the descendants

6

of Ednyfed thus formed a comparatively wealthy and influential clan, referred to in the record evidence as 'Wyrion Eden'.

After the conquest many of these descendants of Ednyfed transferred their allegiance to the English Crown (like other Welsh gentlemen or *uchelwyr* of the time).

Directly descended from Goronwy ap Ednyfed were the rich and powerful 'Tudors of Penmynydd' of southern Anglesey who flourished in the late fourteenth century. They were the five sons of Tudur ap Goronwy (d.1367). Two of the five were dead by about 1382, but the other three brothers were involved in the great rebellion of Owain Glyn Dŵr (1400-15). With the collapse of the rebellion the accumulated wealth and influence of the Tudors of Penmynydd vanished; at least one of the brothers, Rhys ap Tudur, was executed for his part in the rising.

Yet all was not lost. Following the end of the rebellion one of the sons of the Tudors of Penmynydd, Owain ap Maredudd ap Tudur, made his way to the English court and eventually married Henry V's dowager queen, Katherine of Valois, who was of Franco-Bavarian descent. From this marriage of Owen Tudor (as he became known) and Katherine sprang two famous sons, Edmund and Jasper who were created Earls of Richmond and Pembroke respectively by their half-brother King Henry VI. In turn Edmund married the Englishwoman Lady Margaret Beaufort; their son Henry was born in Pembroke Castle in January 1457. The future King Henry VII was thus a direct descendant of Ednyfed Fychan and Gwenllian, although he was but one-quarter Welsh.

From Gruffydd ap Ednyfed also descended a line of powerful landowning squires and officials. The most famous of these men was Sir Rhys ap Gruffydd (d.1356) of Abermarlais. Sir Rhys fought in the Scottish wars of Edward III and also at the Battle of Crecy (1346), and was knighted shortly afterwards. Sir Rhys was 'the wealthiest and most influential figure amongst the native Welsh gentry in the fourteenth century . . . with phenomenally extensive properties in Carmarthenshire and Cardiganshire . . .' (*Dictionary of Welsh Biography*).

Many of these properties remained in the family until the heiress Elizabeth of Abermarlais married Thomas ap Gruffydd, the father of Rhys ap Thomas. In this way much of the wealth and prestige of the line of Gruffydd ap Ednyfed was inherited by Rhys ap Thomas. It was the common family descent from Ednyfed and Gwenllian that later led the poet Lewis Glyn Cothi to write, as we shall see, that Henry Tudor, Jasper Tudor and Rhys ap Thomas were 'men of the same blood'.

Yorkist Victory: the Burgundian Exile

Thomas's marriage to Elizabeth of Abermarlais thus clearly brought new fame and fortune to the family of Gruffydd ap Nicholas. But when Rhys ap Thomas was still a child, these family fortunes began to take an adverse turn. The personal power and authority of Gruffydd ap Nicholas in West Wales was threatened by the rising star of Jasper Tudor, Earl of Pembroke, who was appointed Constable of the key castles of Carmarthen, Aberystwyth, and Carreg Cennen in April 1457.

Jasper has been sent to stiffen the Lancastrian presence in West Wales after the death of Edmund Tudor in Carmarthen in November 1456 (Henry, his son, was a posthumous child). Lewis Glyn Cothi, in an elegy, wrote of his despair on hearing of the death of Edmund, 'brother of King Henry, nephew of the Dauphin, and the son of Owain'. The same poet was soon to write two odes to Jasper praising his Welsh descent and his efforts to rally Wales on behalf of Henry VI. With his royal connections, his youthful energy, and the resources of the rich Lordship of Pembroke, Jasper Tudor was probably more than a military match for the ageing Gruffydd ap Nicholas.

As the prolonged crisis between the houses of York and

Lancaster drifted into civil war by the close of the decade, Gruffydd and his family now gave their support to the Lancastrians. Probably this was because the inherent weakness of the Lancastrian regime still provided an opportunity for Gruffydd ap Nicholas and his family to maintain at least some of their regional power in West Wales.

At any rate, in October 1456 Gruffydd ap Nicholas and his two sons, Owain and Thomas, had been given royal pardons for all treasons, felonies and other crimes committed against the king's peace. Thus it was from this period that dated the family tradition, one that was to play not a little part in Rhys ap Thomas's career, of support for the Lancastrian cause.

Gruffydd ap Nicholas probably died during 1460. He was buried in the famous Church of the Franciscan friars, the Greyfriars or *Cwrt-y-Brodyr*, which stood to the west of the town walls of Carmarthen. Gruffydd's death was soon followed by a complete reversal of the political fortunes of the House of Dinefwr.

This reversal came with the Yorkist victory over Lancastrian forces led by Jasper Tudor at Mortimer's Cross, a strategic road junction north of Hereford, on 2 February 1461. The Yorkists were in turn led by the young Edward, Earl of March, champion of the anti-Lancastrian cause and a formidable military tactician. Jasper Tudor escaped his enemies and fled into Wales to become within a few months a hunted fugitive. Owen Tudor was caught by the Yorkists and beheaded at Hereford.

The Yorkist forces in the west now advanced on London which soon opened its gates to them. The Lancastrian armies in the north, however, still held the person of Henry VI. So on 4 March 1461 the Earl of March was proclaimed and installed as King Edward IV by the Yorkist leaders meeting in London. The new regime was then established beyond doubt with Edward's decisive victory over the main Lancastrian armies at Towton, near York, late in March 1461.

In Wales, the Yorkists moved quickly to consolidate their successes. By early 1462 the sole remaining Lancastrian garrison in the country, apart from Harlech in the north, was Carreg Cennen, held by Owain and Thomas, the sons of Gruffydd ap Nicholas, who had escaped from Mortimer's Cross. After being besieged by strong Yorkist forces, Carreg Cennen surrendered in April 1462; the great masonry fortress in the foothills of the Black Mountains was then partly dismantled to prevent further resistance in the area.

Thomas ap Gruffydd was excluded from holding any further royal office and was clearly in the political wilderness although he retained his estates. He is recorded as holding the lordship of Dinefwr from 1462-65. But under William Herbert of Raglan, Yorkist rule was firmly established in Wales; Herbert was made Justice of South Wales early in the new reign and given many other offices including the constableship of Dinefwr Castle. A close associate of Edward IV, he was made Lord Herbert of Raglan.

Thomas ap Gruffydd with his young son Rhys now went into virtual exile to the Court of Duke Philip of Burgundy. Here Thomas was reputed to have won great renown in the military service of the Duke. The young Rhys, meanwhile, was learning the courtly and martial arts in one of the most civilised societies in Western Europe. It was not until 1467, when Rhys was about eighteen years old, that this young scion of the Blood of the Raven returned with his father to Wales and Abermarlais.

The precise reasons for the return of the father and son to Wales are not known. But it must be remembered that by the mid-1460s the Yorkist regime seemed firmly established in Wales with little apparent hope for a Lancastrian restoration. Thomas ap Gruffydd, moreover, had extensive landed interests in West Wales which must have needed his personal attention. Finally, perhaps, and not least important, there was probably a wish on the part of the exiles to return home to what must have seemed one of the fairest localities in Wales.

Abermarlais

Abermarlais, which was now closely associated with Rhys ap Thomas for the rest of his life, lay in the old Welsh *maenor* of Llansadwrn which was also a parish. Later, Llansadwrn had become a manor in the feudal sense and thus Abermarlais was sometimes referred to as the *caput* or the 'capital demesne' of the manor.

The house, surrounded by parkland, lay on a ridge to the south of the parish. The locality was known as Glasfryn, a name which survives in the area to the present day. Nearby the Marlais stream ran into the Tywi, a confluence which gave the house its name.

Both Llansadwrn and Abermarlais lay in the ancient commote of Maenordeilo, one of the commotes of Cantref Mawr. To the west of Abermarlais lay rolling hill country extending to Talley Abbey. To the east were the hills of Cantref Bychan overlooked by the great scarps of the Black Mountain. Between Abermarlais and the Tywi was the old Roman road which ran from near Hereford and Brecon through Llandovery to Carmarthen. This, then, was the setting of Rhys ap Thomas's home.

A *cywydd*, an alliterative couplet form, written by Lewis Glyn Cothi after the return of Rhys and his father from Burgundy, describes in vivid detail one of the highlights of life at Abermarlais. Entitled 'Rhyfel Plant Thomas yn Abermarlais' (or 'The War of the Thomas Children at Abermarlais') it invokes a medieval tournament attended by Thomas's sons, Morgan, Harry, Rhys and David. Also present were their retainers and other gentry families, the Bassetts, the Rudds and the Mansels, the large company variously armed with

11

The West Wales castles and residences of Sir Rhys ap Thomas

Crown Castles
Carmarthen Castle. Seat of the
Justice and Chamberlain of S. Wales.
Dinefwr Castle
Aberystwyth Castle

Duchy of Lancaster Castles
Carreg Cennen Castle
Kidwelly Castle

Lordship Castles
Newcastle Emlyn
Narberth Castle
Haverfordwest Castle

Residences
Newton House
Abermarlais House
Carew Castle
Weobley Castle
Neuadd Wen (Hunting Lodge)

12

longbows, spears and axes, and the lists were dominated by the raven standards of the Abermarlais family:

I'w llu y bu maes ar ben
Fel y maes fu'i lu Moesen
Ac wyth maner, gwaith menig
A thair bran yn eitha'r brig . . . [1]

('For their host a field was fixed
Like the field that was for the host of Moses
With eight banners in the form of gloves
And three ravens at the very top . . .')

After his return from Burgundy in about 1467, it must have seemed to Rhys ap Thomas, the third son of an active father, that his prospects were limited. But Rhys's fortunes were soon to change decisively.

First, Morgan and David, Rhys's two elder brothers died, pre-deceasing their father Thomas ap Gruffydd. Then Thomas himself either died or was killed in a skirmish. Record evidence seems to indicate that Rhys's father died in 1474. But there is also a strong tradition of a fatal affray in north Wales.

The family history, 'The Life of Rhys ap Thomas', notes that he was killed at Pennal, near Machynlleth. Sir John Wynn (d.1627) also states in his *History of the Gwydir Family* that Thomas ap Gruffydd met his death at Pennal, but in a skirmish with William Herbert's men, perhaps in 1468 at the time of the Yorkist expedition to reduce Harlech Castle. Sir John Wynn's version implies the death of Thomas prior to July 1469, the date of Herbert's own death after the Battle of Banbury.

It also appears that Dafydd Llwyd ap Llywelyn of Mathafarn, the most accomplished and influential prophetic poet of the age, believed that Thomas met his end in north Wales. Mathafarn was near Machynlleth, and Dafydd may have had some local knowledge, for he wrote a *cywydd* to the memory of Thomas ap Gruffydd '*a*

[1] J. Jones & W. Davies, *The Poetical Works of Lewis Glyn Cothi*, 1837, pp. 167-68.

13

laddwyd mewn ymladd yn y maes ym Mhennal' (who was killed in a fight at Pennal).

Dafydd Llwyd states that Thomas was a man of dark features; that he was killed on a Good Friday; he refers to Thomas's connections with Abermarlais and ends his poem by saying that although Thomas is dead, the noble oak is not uprooted and that the raven will be resurrected.[1]

Whatever the precise circumstances of Thomas's death, there is no doubt that it was his third son Rhys who now inherited the family estates at Abermarlais and around Newton. Besides the manor house near Dinefwr built by Rhys's grandfather, the Newton lands probably comprised as well many of the properties accumulated by Gruffydd ap Nicholas in Carmarthenshire and in the Duchy of Lancaster Lordship of Kidwelly.

The ancestral lands which Rhys inherited from his mother, Elizabeth Gruffydd, included not only Abermarlais and the manor of Llansadwrn, but smaller estates at Llanrhystud, Betws Bledrws and Llangybi in Cardiganshire. Llanrhystud certainly, and perhaps the other two Cardiganshire properties, represented gifts from the Princes of Gwynedd to Ednyfed Fychan the Seneschal in circumstances we have related.

Rhys ap Thomas also acquired as part of the Gruffydd inheritance various freehold properties, including several mills in Cantref Mawr, as well as the large manor of Cae Gurwen in the far north of the Lordship of Gower. Here at Neuadd Wen (now Neuadd house), in a sheltered site near the southern slopes of the Black Mountain, Rhys kept a hunting lodge according to the Elizabethan topographer and historian Rice Merrick.

Quite separate from the Gruffydd inheritance were other acquisitions by Rhys ap Thomas in the Lordship of Gower. These included the large Manor of Landimore

[1]For this interesting poem, see W. L. Richards (Ed.), *Gwaith Dafydd Llwyd o Mathafarn*, 1964, pp.132-34.

14

(with sizeable parcels of lands at Rhossili and Llanrhidian) and Weobley Castle and half of its manor. According to Rice Merrick, Rhys acquired Landimore from Sir Roger Vaughan of Tretower who was killed in 1471.

Although he was to hold court for the poets at Newton in the tradition of Gruffydd ap Nicholas, Rhys ap Thomas's chief residence was to remain at Abermarlais (but Carew Castle must have rivalled his mother's home in his affections in later years). Thus it was to Rhys at Thomas at Abermarlais that the celebrated poets Guto'r Glyn and Tudur Aled addressed their *cywyddau*. One of these distinctive poems by Tudur Aled was called, quite simply, 'Caer Farlais', the castle of Marlais. When the Tudor antiquary John Leland visited Abermarlais, probably during 1536-39, he described it as 'a well favoured stone place, motid, now mended and augmented by Sir Rhys ap Thomas'.

It was from Abermalais, therefore, that Rhys ap Thomas controlled his extensive estates in the years following his father's death.

The Landed Magnate

Rhys consolidated his position by taking to wife Eva, daughter and heiress of Henry ap Gwilym of Court Henry in Llangathen parish. (Lewis Dwnn calls her Mably.) Henry was a prominent landowner in the commote of Catheiniog, Cantref Mawr, who may well have been imprisoned by the Lancastrians in Harlech Castle before its capture by William Herbert in 1468. Certainly Henry seems to have found favour with the Yorkists, for during Edwards IV's reign he leased for long periods Dryslwyn Castle and its small town. Rhys's marriage to Eva was therefore politic; it probably brought further property under his control; and it ended a family feud with the builder of Court Henry. Henry ap Gwilym is reputed to have fought (and survived) eight duels with Rhys's father, that formidable soldier Thomas ap Gruffydd.

15

Nevertheless, Rhys remained out of political favour during the later Yorkist period as he was the leading representative of a family whose tradition was Lancastrian. To be sure, Lancastrian hopes had risen as a new round of the civil wars broke out in 1469. Following his defeat at Banbury in July of that year by the forces of Warwick 'the Kingmaker', the chief Welsh Yorkist, William Herbert, Earl of Pembroke, had been put to death. It was Herbert whom Lewis Glyn Cothi had described as Roland to Edward IV's Charlemagne, and as Edward's 'master-lock' in Wales. Later in 1470, Edward himself was forced to flee to the continent, an event followed by the restoration of the Lancastrian Henry VI in October. Jasper Tudor now returned to rally Lancastrian forces in Wales.

But the restoration was far too short-lived for Rhys's family to reap political benefit. Edward IV was the only English king to lose his throne and win it back again personally. Landing in the north during March 1471, Edward routed his enemies at Barnet (14 April) and Tewkesbury (4 May). Both the Lancastrian heir, Prince Edward, and his father, Henry VI, were put to death after Tewkesbury so eliminating the main line of the Lancastrian dynasty. In Wales, Jasper Tudor and his young nephew, Henry, upon whom Lancastrian claims now devolved, escaped from Tenby to the continent. An embryonic Council of Wales was then created by Edward IV in July 1471 which was to extend gradually its supervision over royal and marcher possessions in Wales over the next decade. In Wales, as in England, Yorkist rule was now largely unchallenged until Edward IV's death in 1483.

As his career was to prove, Rhys ap Thomas was as shrewd a realist in the world of contemporary politics as William Herbert or Jasper Tudor. (Rhys was also the true successor to these two men as a major bardic patron.) There can be little doubt that following his father's death, and realising that he was excluded from office, Rhys

16

sought with great, perhaps ruthless, dedication to consolidate and expand his estates.

There is near-contemporary evidence of Rhys's zeal as an estate builder from the Tudor chronicler Elis Gruffydd (d.*c.* 1552) of Llanasa, Flintshire, 'the soldier of Calais'. In his manuscript, 'history' of the world from its creation to his own time, he wrote:

> And indeed many men regarded his death [i.e. the execution of Rhys ap Gruffydd, grandson of Sir Rhys ap Thomas, in 1531] as Divine retribution for the falsehoods of his ancestors, his grandfather, and his great-grandfather, and for their oppression and wrongs. They had many a deep curse from the poor people who were neighbours, for depriving them of their houses, lands, and riches. For I heard the conversation of folk from that part of the country who said that no common people owned land within twenty miles from the dwelling of old Sir Rhys son of Thomas. If he desired such lands he would appropriate them without payment or thanks, and the disinherited doubtless cursed him, his children and his grandchildren, which curses in the opinion of many men fell on the family, according to the old proverb which says—the children of lies are uprooted, and after oppression comes a long death to the oppressors.
>
> (N.L.W. Mostyn MS 158)

Elis Gruffydd's comment that no freeholder within twenty miles of Rhys ap Thomas was safe from his predatory attention has rung down the centuries. Yet Rhys's acquisitiveness should be seen in its historical context and thus perhaps two comments are opposite.

Firstly, the fifteenth century was one of the most complex periods in Welsh history. One of its primary phenomena was the sometimes headlong acquisition of estates and property by a new landed class. This historic movement had its origins perhaps as early as the thirteenth century in a few cases. But it certainly gathered decisive momentum with the decline of collective medieval institutions caused by the Black Death and the great revolt of Owain Glyn Dŵr. Both the manorial system in Wales and the age-old Welsh tribal system of common land ownership by the kindred were thus on the way out in the face of a new rising class of landed squires. A further factor was the weakness of English government in Wales under Henry VI, compounded by the civil wars between 1455-85. The net result was an ever-greater accumulation of power and influence by an increasingly autonomous Welsh gentry class.

According to Glanmor Williams,

> The rapid disintegration of the old order in the first half of the fifteenth century enabled the up-and-coming families to build their fortunes much more quickly than would otherwise have been the case. A decisive phase in the origins of the landed families who dominated pre-industrial Wales is almost always to be traced to the first half of the fifteenth century ... So fluid were the political and economic conditions at the outset that the most successful families could hope to come to the very top, and that within a generation almost ... [1]

In this historic process, the family of Gruffydd ap Nicholas were pre-eminent in West Wales, although others such as the Mansels of Oxwich in Gower were well to the fore. The ambitions which characterised Gruffydd's activities, which we have already noted, were thus to descend in full measure to Rhys ap Thomas who was to become the leading Welsh champion of this new landed class. But it should be stressed that Rhys was only the most prominent of these aspiring Welsh estate builders.

Rhys ap Thomas's single-minded concern with his estates was but one aspect of the general resurgence in the vitality and self-confidence of leading Welsh families in the fifteenth century. Here the kinship link was all-important. J. E. Caerwyn Williams has noted that perhaps the best key to the 'unbounded ambition' and the 'incessant strife' that attended the rise of this landed élitc

> is a proper understanding of the family and its role, for the family's prominence, extension, and its aggrandisement come

[1] *The Welsh Church from Conquest to Reformation*, 1976 ed., pp.251-52.

as close to being universal motives for the wide variety of aristocratic activity as any other single force. There was the added emphasis on possessions, on lineage, on blood ties, and on the desire to maintain the family identity across the generations . . .[1]

The emergence of a rising landed class displaying intense family pride was of course common to both Wales and England at this time. But in Wales many members of this group were increasingly involved, from a variety of motives, in the attainment of long-held national aspirations. With Edward IV's death in April 1483, and the subsequent usurpation of the throne by his brother, Duke Richard of Gloucester, a time for decision approached for many influential Welshmen.

Much of the military skill and physical energy that had been dissipated in internecine feuding in Wales since the time of Owain Glyn Dŵr was now to be channelled into a great dynastic cause henceforth uniquely associated with Wales. Through his family's prestige and its bardic connections, through his own military training and the resources of his extensive estates (especially as a cavalry training ground), Rhys ap Thomas was especially qualified to assume leadership. For not long after the usurpation of Richard III, Rhys ap Thomas became involved in the covert movement to replace the usurper by Henry Tudor.

In this movement, Rhys was eventually to play the part of Henry Tudor's chief Welsh supporter. After 1485, Rhys was to play many other roles. He was to become a loyal, powerful subject of the first two Tudor kings, a leading Crown administrator in Wales, and an outstanding bardic patron. But in all these activities Rhys ap Thomas's fame was ultimately underwritten by his power and authority as a great landed magnate. We must now ask, how did Rhys come to ally himself with Henry Tudor?

[1] A. O. H. Jarman & G. R. Hughes (eds.), *A Guide to Welsh Literature*, Vol. II, 1979, p.235.

Chapter II
Rhys ap Thomas and Henry Tudor
1483-1485

Rhys ap Thomas came to maturity at a time critical in the history of both Wales and England. The interaction of events in both countries between 1483 and 1485 was to have profound consequences in that the two peoples were to be drawn together in a way that had not seemed possible before. In these events which culminated at Bosworth Field, Rhys ap Thomas was to play an important role.

The Prophetic Tradition
To understand these developments we should remember that in the mid-fifteenth century the ancient prophecies that had governed Welsh national aspirations for many centuries seemed close to fulfilment in the view of many Welsh people.

These prophecies went back to the beginnings of Welsh poetry at the time of Taliesin (c. 6th century A.D.). At the heart of the Welsh prophetic tradition was the concept of a hero-king, an Owain, a Cadwaladr, or an Arthur who would appear as a 'Son of Prophecy' ('Mab Darogan') and lead the Welsh to dominion again over the whole of the British island. Prophecy took many forms, and drew on many sources of inspiration, Christian and pre-Christian, but essentially it was a message of hope in that it looked forward to a time when the present unhappy circumstances of a conquered people would change for the better.

For the Welsh people the prophecies were eventually given a definitive, immensely influential form in Geoffrey of Monmouth's *Historia Regum Brittaniae* (or the *History of the Kings of Britain*) which appeared in about 1136. Although we cannot be certain, it seems possible that Geoffrey's origins may have been Breton. He

20

was probably brought up in a Norman-Welsh environment at Monmouth, and there is an unmistakeable preoccupation in his work with the Roman legionary fortress of Caerleon-on-Usk not far away.

The *British History*, as it is often known, was a powerful, emotional and imaginative work which related the story of the Welsh royal descent from Brutus, great-grandson of the Trojan hero, Aeneas, of the marvellous acts of the British kings, including Arthur, and of the memorable, patriotic prophecies of the wizard Merlin. The key passage in the *British History* which would continue to move Welsh hearts and minds was the prophecy spoken by an Angelic voice to Cadwladr the Blessed, 'the last king of Britain', reminding him that 'the British people would occupy the island again at some time in the future, once the appointed moment should come'.

Cadwaladr (d. 664) was an historical king, from whom, through Rhodri the Great (d.878) descended the rulers of both Gwynedd and Deheubarth in the early middle ages. These rulers were snuffed out in the thirteenth century. But despite the death of Llywelyn 'the Last' of Gwynedd in 1282 and Owain Glyn Dŵr's lost, last bid for independence, there was a significant revival of Welsh patriotic feeling in the fifteenth century.

This revival was inseparable from the memories of Glyn Dŵr's achievements, combined with intensified anti-English feelings. These sentiments were now crystallised by classical poets, often in the *cywydd brud* form which foretold the triumph of the heirs of Brutus. The poets, however, no longer seemed to envisage an independent Wales, but rather the triumph of their patrons within the existing political system.

Verses by such famous poets as Dafydd Llwyd, Lewis Glyn Cothi, and Guto'r Glyn were often directed to influential patrons such as Jasper Tudor and William Herbert, men whose every military campaign in Wales would have been known to Rhys ap Thomas. Of great

21

importance is the fact that these poems were often envisaged by authors and patrons alike as propaganda in the civil wars between the houses of York and Lancaster.

Many Welshmen, high and low, had come to believe that this profound dynastic crisis for the English monarchy was a supreme opportunity for the advancement of Welsh interests generally, irrespective of the rival claims of York and Lancaster. The poets often attempted to get backing for Welsh leaders, quite apart from whether these champions were Yorkists or Lancastrians. The bards also tended to describe the civil wars as a contest between the Welsh and the English.

During the Wars of the Roses, control of Wales and the Marches was of great strategic importance to the warring English factions. This was a factor which thus maximised the military leverage which Welshmen could exert. E. D. Jones has written that 'at no time in its history did Wales play a more decisive part in English politics than in the quarter of a century between 1460 and 1485, and the poets were fully conscious of it . . .'[1]

Some idea of the Welsh hopes raised by the crisis of the civil wars may be seen in a famous *cywydd* written to William Herbert by Guto'r Glyn in which the poet called on the Yorkist leader to unite the country:

> Dwg Forgannwg a Gwynedd
> Gwna'n un o Gonwy i Nedd.
> O digia Lloegr a'i dugiaid,
> Cymru a dry yn dy raid.[2]

('Make Glamorgan and Gwynedd, from Conwy to Neath, a united whole. And should England and her dukes resent it, Wales will rally to thy side.')

Rhys ap Thomas was a natural beneficiary of all these concepts when the time came for him to join Henry Tudor in 1485.

---

[1] 'Wales in Fifteenth Century Politics', in *Wales Through the Ages*, Vol. 1, 1975 ed., p.186.
[2] *Gwaith Guto'r Glyn*, 1939, p.144.

22

March and Principality

Guto'r Glyn's passionate appeal for Welsh unity reminds us that ever since the advent of the middle ages Wales had been a divided country. Following the Norman conquest of England the invaders quickly advanced westwards to the Welsh borders and soon created a network of castles and independent lordships which stretched from the vicinity of Chester to Chepstow and thence westwards to Pembroke. By about 1100 the March or Marches of Wales had come into existence.

To the west and north of the March there remained the Welsh principalities of Gwynedd, Powys and Deheubarth which were gradually conquered by Anglo-Norman forces over the next two-hundred years. With the death of Llywelyn ap Gruffydd of Gwynedd in 1282, and the execution of his brother the following year, Welsh independence was at an end.

A far-reaching administrative settlement of the conquered lands in Wales, North and South, was then promulgated in Edward I's Statute of Rhuddlan (1284). This ordinance created what was to become known as the royal Principality of Wales which was a feudal property of the Crown quite distinct from both the March and the realm of England. Thus the fundamental division of Wales into two remained until 1536 when the entire system was swept away by Henry VIII.

A few details of the Edwardian settlement are relevant here for as we have seen Rhys ap Thomas's father and grandfather were closely concerned in the workings of royal administration in West Wales. Rhys himself was eventually to hold the two chief Crown offices in the area. For most of his life, whether in or out of office, the royal administration in West Wales, and the affairs of the adjoining Marcher Lordships, would have been of constant concern to Rhys.

Under the Statute of 1284, the Principality of Wales was divided into two entities. In north-west Wales, usually known as the 'Principality of North Wales', the three newly-created royal counties of Anglesey, Caernarfon and Merioneth were administered from Caernarfon Castle. In the south-west, the royal counties of Carmarthen and Cardigan, the 'Principality of South Wales', were ruled from Carmarthen Castle.[1] The royal County of Carmarthen, when it was fully consolidated, was only half the size of the county of the same name that existed from 1536 to 1974. In north-east Wales, the shire of Flint was put under the King's Justice of Chester.

The royal government in each part of the Principality was headed by a Justice or Justiciar who held the supreme executive and judicial powers analagous to those held by a Viceroy. The Chamberlain headed the Exchequer, while the Sheriff was an important subordinate law officer. Local administration on the commotal level was left to Welsh officials. English criminal law was brought into the Principality, but Welsh civil law was allowed.

After 1301 the Principality was vested in the King's eldest son as Prince of Wales and there was a number of such holders of the Principality over the next two centuries. Throughout the period of the Principality, the March remained of course as a mosaic of separate lordships. But as time passed many of the Marcher lordships passed to the Crown for a variety of reasons. By 1536, therefore, the King was the most important Marcher lord.

All the administrative anomalies of a Wales divided were exacerbated in the fifteenth century by weak royal authority, the concomitant breakdown of law and order, and diminished revenues in Principality and March alike. As we have seen in the case of Gruffydd ap Nicholas, government by deputy became quite common. The absence of one judicial authority helped the rise of lawlessness as wrongdoers could escape from Principality

[1] For a comprehensive account of royal government in the South, see R. A. Griffiths, *The Principality of Wales in the Later Middle Ages: I: South Wales 1277-1536*, 1972.

24

to March and *vice versa.* Another important element in the decline of public order was the 'Redeeming of the Sessions', the practice by which in both Principality and March higher courts were cancelled for an arranged fee from the community. In this way judicial income was stabilised but at the cost of further disorder.

All the cumulative shortcomings of this administrative system had led to the broad national support for Owain Glyn Dŵr which we have already noted. The rebellion had been defeated but the new patriotism kindled by Owain lived on. Now, in a fresh dynastic crisis, the bards discerned a new Son of Prophecy in the person of Henry Tudor. Between 1483 and 1485 Rhys ap Thomas was to emerge as Henry's chief ally in Wales. Yet Rhys's enlistment to Henry's cause was not a simple matter.

Rhys meets Buckingham

Despite the anomalies of government in Wales, compounded by the endemic lawlessness of the time, the Yorkist regime seemed to have consolidated itself in the country by the early 1480s. There was little hope of a Lancastrian resurgence. All this was changed by the sudden, premature death of Edward IV on 9 April 1483. In the prolonged crisis that followed, and which was only resolved at Bosworth Field, Rhys ap Thomas was now destined to play an increasingly central role. Here was a situation where Welsh national sentiment, English dynastic politics, and Rhys's own interests overlapped. But Rhys was not hasty in declaring his hand.

Following King Edward's death the throne passed to his twelve year old son who became Edward V. The former King's younger brother, Richard, Duke of Gloucester, was made Protector and soon moved to eliminate any opposition. Gloucester put Edward V in the Tower together with his younger brother, Richard, Duke of York, who was next in succession. On 26 June 1483 Gloucester usurped the throne as Richard III; 'the Princes in the

Tower' were seen no more and were generally believed murdered on Richard's orders.

During the late summer of 1483 an opposition against Richard III began to form and soon adopted the objective of replacing the king with Henry Tudor, Earl of Richmond. The movement was comprised of Yorkists loyal to the memory of Edward IV and his sons, some remaining Lancastrians, and others who disliked Richard III's violent and illegal methods. This opposition was probably initiated by Henry Tudor's influential mother, Lady Margaret Beaufort, who gave her son his claim to the throne by virtue of her descent from Edward III. Although his claim was flawed by descent from the illegitimate Beaufort line, Richard III's methods had transformed Henry Tudor from an obscure exile into a strong claimant to the throne.

Henry's part-Welsh ancestry was to be vital in mobilising support for his cause in Wales. As we have related, Henry's grandfather Owen Tudor was descended ultimately from Welsh royal stock and the Trojan line. Owen Tudor's two sons, the Earls of Richmond and Pembroke, had added further lustre to the family names as Lancastrian standard bearers in Wales. 'Two noblemen from Troy and Greece, the root is good', were the opening lines of a prophetic or vaticinal *cywydd* by the influential poet Dafydd Nanmor written as early as 1453. It was a theme the poets were often to repeat during the next decades in relation to the Tudor family.

Following Henry's birth in Pembroke Castle in 1457 the young child was probably brought up in this great fortress. But after the Yorkist victories of 1461, Henry was taken into the home of William Herbert, the Yorkist leader in Wales, and grew up at Herbert's home at Raglan Castle, incidentally a great centre of bardic patronage. In yet another round of the Wars of the Roses, Herbert was killed in 1469 and the following year saw a brief Lancastrian restoration. But in 1471 Edward IV returned to his throne

26

in what seemed a final Yorkist victory. Henry and his uncle Jasper then fled from Tenby to Brittany. For both, years of exile and uncertainty followed. But now, in 1483, all this seemed to be coming to an end.

Once the conspiracy against Richard III was launched, Rhys ap Thomas was approached. Rhys seemed the logical choice as a leading Welsh supporter of the anti-Richard movement. He could deploy relatively large forces from his extensive estates, especially cavalry forces, and he was a trained soldier. He had an intimate knowledge of the topography and the military potential of South Wales as his later route to join Henry Tudor shows.

In addition, Rhys probably disliked being in the political wilderness under the Yorkists. A change of regime would probably bring him the power and the prominence that his father and grandfather had enjoyed, and would also restore in general the family political fortunes. Evidently, too, Rhys possessed an innate skill as a conspirator for Richard III was deceived as to Rhys's ultimate intentions until the Raven was actually on his way to rendezvous with Henry Tudor in August 1485.

According to the family history, 'The Life of Sir Rhys ap Thomas' (see below), the conspirators used as their intermediary with Rhys the distinguished Welsh physician and astronomer Lewis of Caerleon. He was Lady Margaret Beaufort's doctor and had also acted some years previously as Rhys ap Thomas's tutor. He was thus able to travel to Abermarlais unsuspected. But it appears that late in 1483 Lewis was jailed by Richard III (to be released and rewarded after Bosworth Field). Lewis also acted at this stage of the conspiracy as the go-between linking Lady Margaret with Edward IV's widow, Queen Elizabeth Woodville, who had been drawn into the plot as an important participant.

Lewis was useful in helping to reconcile Rhys with his regional rival the Duke of Buckingham for the men were separated by 'a deadlie quarrel'. Henry Stafford, second

Duke of Buckingham, was descended from Edward III, had many Lancastrian connections, and held amongst his extensive properties the Marcher Lordships of Brecon, Hay and Huntington. Buckingham had been involved in Richard III's *coup d'état* and had been generously rewarded with the posts of Justice and Chamberlain of both North and South Wales as well as with the custody of many other royal castles in Wales and the March. But for reasons of his own, never entirely clear, Buckingham turned against Richard III and thus initially an independent centre of conspiracy existed at Brecon Castle. Buckingham then aligned himself with the main opposition to Richard III, so giving the subsequent revolt his name.

Rhys met Buckingham at Trecastle, the little town near the western border of the Lordship of Brecon, in order to smooth over their differences. But Rhys was not involved in the subsequent rising which in any case was located in the south and west of England. Rhys was probably reluctant to act in a rebellion which if successful would have strengthened even further Buckingham's position in the region. According to the family history noted above, Rhys foresaw 'an alteration in the state' but that was all.

In the event, Buckingham's revolt of October 1483 was a fiasco. The Duke moved north-eastwards from Brecon towards the Severn crossings, but the operation collapsed through bad weather and the reluctance of Buckingham's Welsh tenants to fight for him. According to the historian Polydore Vergil (see below), these Welsh forces abandoned Buckingham 'whom he as a sore and hard-dealing man had brought to the field against their wills and without any lust to fight for him, rather by rigorous commandment than for money'. In addition, shortly after the revolt began, Buckingham's base of Brecon Castle was captured by Sir Thomas Vaughan of Tretower and his kinsmen. The Vaughans were Yorkist supporters while Sir Thomas's father, Sir Roger Vaughan, had been summarily executed on Jasper Tudor's orders at Chepstow in 1471.

As part of the revolt, a number of risings had been planned for the south and west of England, but these actions were badly coordinated and were soon mopped by Richard's security forces. The bad weather also meant that Henry Tudor's expedition from northern Britanny to the west of England failed to make a proper landfall, fortunately for Henry. Buckingham was captured and then executed at Salisbury on 2 November 1483.

Both Henry Tudor and Rhys ap Thomas had thus learnt the necessity of caution, timing, coordination and above all secrecy in dealing with their dangerous adversary. Rhys ap Thomas has taken the right decision in not backing Buckingham's revolt.

Henry and the French Court

Following the collapse of Buckingham's revolt, Rhys ap Thomas bided his time. A number of Henry Tudor's supporters, both Lancastrians and dissident Yorkists, quickly made their way to Brittany so forming a community of loyal exiles around Henry. At Rennes Cathedral on Christmas Day 1483 the exiles pledged their allegiance to Henry who swore that once he had won the throne of England he would marry Elizabeth of York, Edward IV's eldest daughter, so linking and reconciling the house of York and Lancaster.

Richard III meanwhile stepped up his defences against a second Tudor expedition combined with a rising in England and Wales. Captured adherents of Buckingham's revolt were executed. But the King's methods were also conciliatory. Lady Margaret Beaufort's estates were put under the custody of her husband Thomas, Lord Stanley. But as Richard III did not wish to alienate Stanley or his brother, Sir William, who were powerful landed magnates in the north-west and on the Welsh borders, Lady Margaret escaped lightly from her involvement in

Buckingham's revolt. The movement against Richard III thus remained in being and the Stanleys were now brought into its ambience.

Richard also attempted to buy support through the use of royal patronage. A number of Welsh gentry were given annuities and Rhys ap Thomas himself was given such an annuity of forty marks. Richard also initiated military counter-measures against a Tudor landing. Naval patrols in the Channel kept a watchful eye, and a system of coastal defences, including warning beacons, was organised on the south coasts of both England and Wales. There were special precautions in West Wales where a number of strategically-sited castles were put into a state of readiness under a loyal Yorkist, Richard Williams. These included Pembroke, along with Haverfordwest, Tenby, and Cilgerran on the Teifi which guarded access from the south to Cardiganshire.

During 1484 the King put pressure on Duke Francis of Brittany to repatriate Henry Tudor. The King's efforts were helped by the Duke's illness and the temporary passing of effective power to the ducal treasurer, Pierre Landois. Henry learnt of these moves and just in time fled to France along with Jasper Tudor. Duke Francis then recovered his health and many of Henry's loyal supporters followed him to France.

The key to a new expedition against Richard III now lay with the French court of Charles VIII. Real power was held by Charles's elder sister, Anne of Beaujeu, who dominated the Council of Regency. It was 'a cardinal objective' of French policy 'to ensure that Britanny in due course should become part of the Kingdom of France. It followed that if Henry Tudor could be used to contribute to that end, he would so be used'.[1]

Henry was thus welcomed by the French court where he was seen as a potential instrument to offset any alliance

[1] S. B. Chrimes, *Henry VII*, 1972, pp.31-32.

30

between Richard III and Britanny. There was no immediate French commitment to back Henry, that came later. But preparations continued across the Channel in England to receive Henry. As the time for the final decisions grew near, so Rhys ap Thomas's role as a potential Tudor supporter acquired an entirely new significance.

For the final phases of the movement against Richard III and the subsequent Bosworth campaign two important sources, one reliable, one not so reliable, should be briefly mentioned. The general movement of events, and the development of the conspiracy against Richard is clearly depicted in Polydore Vergil's *English History*. The author, an accomplished and learned Papal diplomat, came to England in 1502 and soon became a friend of Henry VII.

Henry encouraged Polydore Vergil to write a modern, full-scale history of England on which the Italian began work in about 1506. For the events of 1483-85 Polydore had the help of a number of surviving participants, including almost certainly the king. Time has shown that Polydore Vergil's account is generally accurate. While his history is not neutral in that he took a broadly favourable view of the coming of the Tudors, he remains a reliable historian of great value.

Our second source is the family history, 'The Life of Sir Rhys ap Thomas', which was probably written by Henry Rice of Dynevor or Dinefwr (d.c. 1651) to clear the family name tarnished by the execution of Rhys ap Gruffydd, Rhys ap Thomas's grandson, in 1531.[2] The *Life* is not always reliable in that it presents an eulogistic, undeviatingly favourable view of Rhys's loyalty to Henry Tudor from 1483 onwards. But as we have seen, Rhys was hesitant and calculating, and in any case he had to move very carefully before committing himself irrevocably to Henry. In his entry on Rhys ap Thomas in the *Dictionary*

[2] The family name was anglicized to Rice in the mid-sixteenth century and changed back to Rhys in 1916.

31

of National Biography (vol. 48, 1896) Sir John Lloyd considered that the *Life* 'depends too much on tradition to be altogether trustworthy, yet contains much important information'.

Despite Henry's flight to France and the inevitable delays in mounting his expedition, Richard III's political credibility weakened during 1484 and early 1485. The King suffered a severe blow when his son, Edward, died on 8 April 1484, aged eleven. A year later on 11 March 1485 his wife, Queen Anne, died. Richard did not marry again, and did not sponsor the marriage of his surviving nieces, the daughters of Edward IV. The King had thus reached what S. B. Chrimes, Henry VIII's biographer, has aptly called 'a dynastic impasse'. The corollary was that Richard III placed ever-greater emphasis on vigilance and preparedness to defeat Henry Tudor's coming expedition.

Rhys joins the Conspiracy

Despite Richard III's annuity to Rhys, the King remained suspicious of the Welshman and asked for a hostage in the form of Rhys's son, Gruffydd (d.1521). Gruffydd was the son of Rhys's first marriage to Eva (or Mably), the daughter of Henry ap Gwilym. (Rhys ap Thomas was married for the second time to Janet, daughter of Thomas Mathew of Radyr; she was the widow of Thomas Stradling of St. Donats. Janet died in 1535 and was buried in the Carmarthen Greyfriars.) According to the family *Life*, Rhys was able to parry the royal demand for his son by assuring Richard that Henry of Richmond 'must resolve with himself to make his entrance and irruption over my bellie'. Hence the apocryphal story that Rhys stood under Mullock bridge between Dale and Haverfordwest as Henry and his men passed overhead *en route* for Bosworth.

Richard III's suspicions of Rhys ap Thomas were not misplaced. Following Henry's flight from Brittany to France the planning for a new expedition against Richard

III took on an entirely new strategic aspect, one in which Rhys's involvement was imperative.

Henry Tudor now intended to land near Dale at the northern entrance to Milford Haven. He would then march north-eastwards through Haverfordwest, Cardigan and along the west coast of Wales to Machynlleth. The way would then lie forward through the Cambrian mountains to Shrewsbury and the heart of England for the final showdown with Richard III. This route would circumvent Pembroke and the direct route to England through Carmarthen which was well-guarded by Richard's men. The slightly more northerly route through Brecon and Hereford was also considered too risky. In addition, West Wales was an excellent landing-place in that its sympathies were generally Lancastrian; Jasper Tudor was of course still the titular Lancastrian Earl of Pembroke.

As the most powerful magnate in West Wales, Rhys ap Thomas's support was necessary to ensure Henry's unimpeded progress through Wales. He could fend off Yorkist forces, he could mobilise allies and sympathisers, and above all he could arrange a firm rendezvous with Henry so that their combined army could then confront Richard III. How was Rhys drawn into the conspiracy?

According to the family *Life*, Rhys was approached by John Morgan of Tredegar, who later in 1496 became Bishop of St David's, and his brother the distinguished lawyer Morgan of Kidwelly. A relative of the brothers, Evan Morgan, had fled to Brittany to join Henry after the collapse of Buckingham's revolt. Another member of the Welsh side of the conspiracy was Arnold Butler of Coedcanlas near Pembroke. The Abbot of Talley was involved to ease Rhys's conscience over his rebellion. The object of these intrigues—and we may easily imagine the secret meetings and the comings and goings in West Wales—was to ensure that Rhys delivered to Henry Tudor 'the keys of that part of the kingdom'.

With his commitment to Henry Tudor, Rhys now enlisted a network of friends and kinsmen, organised a system of warning beacons along a line of march, and most important of all mobilized a force of 'full 2000 horse well-manned and well-armed'. A rearguard of 500 men was earmarked in case of disaster.

The subsequent successful coordination of forces from all over Wales—in an era when modern roads did not exist—strongly suggests a detailed, prearranged plan in the preparation of which Rhys must have played a leading part. Whatever the partisan origins of the *Life*, referred to above, these military details involving the organization—and subsequent execution—of Rhys's plan to support Henry Tudor ring true.

As these preparations in Wales went ahead, the French government now decided to back a Tudor expedition against Richard III as a means of offsetting a possible understanding between England and Brittany. Eventually, as Henry's final preparations at the mouth of the Seine neared completion in the summer of 1485, good news reached him from Wales. John Morgan reported that both Rhys ap Thomas and the Cheshire landowner John Savage (d.1492) 'were wholly given to Earl Henry's affairs'. Rhys was described as 'a man of great service and valiant' (Polydore Vergil).

John Morgan also reported that Reginald Bray, a stalwart of the anti-Richard conspiracy, had collected 'no small sum of money' to pay the troops. He urged Henry to launch his expedition as soon as possible. As he was understandably anxious to avoid further delay, Henry now completed his arrangements and decided to sail for Wales at the beginning of August. The die was cast.

Of Rhys ap Thomas's motives in joining Henry's risky enterprise we can only speculate. Before his landing in Wales Henry Tudor had sent letters in semi-regal style to potential Welsh supporters promising to free them from their servitudes. One such letter was amongst the archives of Rhys's family confiscated after the execution of Rhys ap Gruffydd in 1531, but later destroyed by fire. An example of one of these letters is found in *The History of the Gwydir Family* by Sir John Wynn (d.1627), for Henry had written to one of his ancestors, John ap Maredudd.

In practice neither Rhys ap Thomas nor the emerging Welsh landed class he represented were much constrained by such restrictions. Yet the general claims of Welsh national sentiment which Henry Tudor inspired may well have played a part in Rhys's decision to support Henry. The kinship link with the Tudors is another reason why Rhys may have rallied to Henry in 1485.

Much more likely as factors in Rhys's commitment to Henry Tudor are the elements of ambition, realism and calculation that characterised Rhys's father and grand-father as they fought for and won regional supremacy in West Wales in the mid-fifteenth century. In the Yorkist period, as we have seen, Rhys was in the political wilderness. But with the advent of Henry Tudor, Rhys probably saw a potential royal guarantor of the long-term interests of himself and his family. His judgement in 1485 proved correct and Rhys succeeded to offices never held by Gruffydd ap Nicholas, even if Gruffydd's defiance of the Crown was no longer possible.

The Poets Speak

Rhys ap Thomas's involvement in the preparations for Henry's landing in the summer of 1485 may not have been solely military. He was the third generation of his family who patronised the bards and eventually he became the greatest patron in Wales.

Although the record evidence available is silent on this point, it would be entirely consistent with Rhys's record if he were involved as a patron in the great bardic programme of preparing Wales for Henry Tudor's landing. The poem by Lewis Glyn Cothi noted below is suggestive of such involvement. At least thirty-five poets were active in this bardic campaign. Moreover, as the Tudor landing approached, so the expectations of the poets rose to a climax. The place of the landing was no secret to some of the bards.

Thus Dafydd Llwyd of Mathafarn, the prophetic poet and seer, declared his intention to look towards Mynyw (Menevia), to scan the coast from Aberystwyth to Bristol, for the coming of a tall Welshman. Dafydd Gorlech also prophesied the arrival in Menevia of a bull with a golden shield. Some poets were even more specific. When a hundred thousand would land in Milford, sang Robin Ddu, the English would flee. Another poet, Ieuan ap Gruffydd Leiaf, wrote that once the landing was made at Milford, a gift of cattle would be sent from Gwynedd, no doubt as a means of supplying the expedition.

As Henry's landing became imminent, Dafydd Llwyd of Mathafarn wrote a majestic ode to St David in which the protection of the patron saint was sought for the long awaited *Mab Darogan*. The seer envisaged an apocalyptic clash of arms in which the mole, Richard III, would be destroyed. The poem ended with a strong call for Welsh support for the deliverer: 'Enemies will meet in the field this year, before the end of September; every wide land, all of our race, every district, everybody for St David ...' ('Gelynion a drig eleni—ym maes/Cyn diwedd mis Medi/Pob tir maith, pawb o'n iaith ni,/Pob tuedd, pawb at Dewi ...')[1]

Lewis Glyn Cothi, the faithful laureate of the House of Dinefwr, was also active in the weeks before the landing in Mynyw. His emotional and evocative *cywydd* to Jasper Tudor, 'the black bull' of the prophetic poetry, was expressed in terms of mounting impatience:

[1] G. A. Williams, 'The Bardic Road to Bosworth: A Welsh View of Henry Tudor', *Trans. Hon. Soc. of Cymmrodorion*, 1986, pp.26-27.

Siaspar, pa ddarpar yr wyd?
pa fôr y mae d'angorau?
pa bryd (pa hyd y'n hoedir?)
Y tarw du, y troi i dir?[1]

('Jasper, what preparations do you make?
In what seas are your anchors?
When, O black bull, will you turn to land?
How long shall we have to wait?')

Lewis clearly expected Rhys ap Thomas to be one of the mainstays of the coming campaign and urged Jasper Tudor to join forces with the Raven:

Cymer di wŷr Cymru, d'ach
Y fran yn dy gyfrinach

('Welshman know thy stock
Take the raven into thy confidence.')

This exhortation was soon complied with as Rhys ap Thomas met Henry Tudor and as the prophecies now began to come true in the Bosworth campaign.

---

[1] *The Poetical Works of Lewis Glyn Cothi*, 1837, op.cit., pp.477-79.

Chapter III
Rhys's Road to Bosworth

On 1 August 1485 Henry's expeditionary forces sailed from Harfleur for Wales. The force included about four-thousand French troops, both mercenaries and seasoned professionals paid by the King of France. Some five-hundred English exiles accompanied Henry. There was a detachment of the Scots Guard of the French King, as well as some Breton adventurers. The French chronicler Commines writes that the French had also given Henry some artillery. Even so, the odds seemed stacked against Henry in his risky bid for the throne.

The Landing in Wales

Henry's men landed at Mill Bay, a sheltered cove at the northern entrance of Milford Haven, immediately east of St Ann's Head, on the evening of 7 August. Henry is reported to have kissed the soil of Pembrokeshire, made the sign of the Cross and to have told his men to follow him in the name of the Lord and of St George. The troops then advanced to Dale, nearly two miles away, for the night. Caution was indicated because Richard III's forces had been stationed at Dale the previous winter.

Moreover, Richard's agents must have seen the landing, probably from the Angle area on the opposite side of the Haven from Mill Bay. We know this because as soon as 11 August, from near Nottingham, Richard III issued orders to array his own forces. His enemies had landed 'at Nangle, besides Milford Haven', the King wrote, possibly referring to a diversionary landing by Henry's men.

From Dale, Henry quickly advanced to Haverfordwest the next morning. Here he was well received by the populace. Arnold Butler of Coedcanlas brought some men

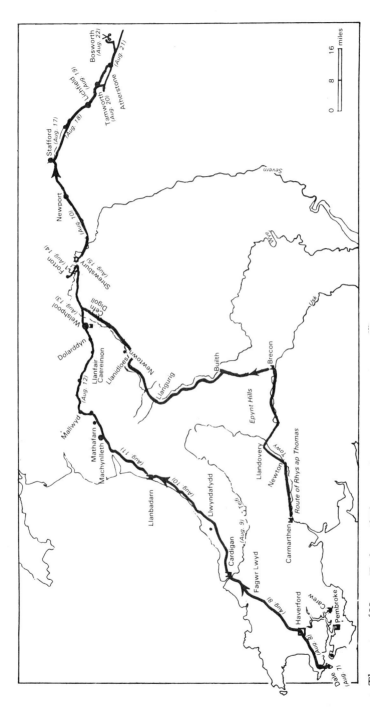

The routes of Henry Tudor and Rhys ap Thomas to Bosworth Field, August 1485 (after William Rees)

to join him. A swift advance to pick up further support was now essential as Henry's little army was at its most vulnerable in these first days of the campaign. From Haverfordwest, and without a long halt, Henry pushed north-eastwards over the Preseli hills towards Cardigan. That night, 8 August, Henry is supposed to have slept at the homestead of Fagwr Lwyd, on the northern slopes of the Preseli Hills not far from the Cardigan road.

These early days of the campaign must have been particularly worrying for Henry. There were rumours at Haverfordwest that Rhys ap Thomas (Polydore Vergil calls him Richard) and John Savage, pledged supporters, were loyal to Richard III. There were also fears about the allegiance of Sir Walter Herbert, another supposed ally, but who was now rumoured, falsely, to be at Carmarthen with hostile forces. He was the second son of William Herbert, Henry's former guardian and the first Yorkist Earl of Pembroke. But not all the news was bad between Haverfordwest and Cardigan. Richard Griffith, of a west Wales landed family and 'a man of his parentage' came to join Henry as did John Morgan. This was a relative of Henry's supporter of the same name who had helped him by enlisting Rhys ap Thomas to the cause.

About this time Henry sent a message to his mother Lady Margaret Beaufort and the two Stanleys, Lord Stanley and Sir William, that he intended to cross the Severn and advance through Shropshire to London. The tension and confusion of these days is well represented by Shakespeare:

Lord Stanley: . . . But tell me where is princely Richmond now?

Sir Christopher Urswick: At Pembroke or at Ha'rford-west in Wales.

Stanley: What men of name resort to him?

Urswick: Sir Walter Herbert, a renowned soldier,
Sir Gilbert Talbot, Sir William Stanley,

40

Oxford, redoubted Pembroke, Sir James Blunt,
And Rice ap Thomas with a valiant crew;
And many others of great name and worth;
and towards London do they bend their power,
If by the way they be not fought withal . . .

(Richard III, IV, v, 1.9-18)

From Cardigan, the march continued northwards probably through Llwyndafydd, near today's Newquay, where Henry is reputed to have spent the night of 9 August. His army advanced under the Red Dragon standard of Cadwaladr, later described by the Tudor chronicler Edward Hall as 'a red fiery dragon beaten upon green and white sarcenet'. By about 11 August, perhaps a little later, Henry was at Mathafarn, four miles east of Machynlleth, the home of Dafydd Llwyd the poet. His route now lay eastwards from here through the heart of the Cambrian mountains to the Severn and Shrewsbury. If all went well Henry hoped to meet Rhys ap Thomas and other Welsh contingents on the eastern flank of the Welsh mountains near Welshpool.

Stogging them to Shrewsbury

Polydore Vergil gives the impression that during these early days of the march through Wales, Henry was uncertain as to Rhys ap Thomas's intentions. Besides the earlier rumour that Rhys and John Savage were loyal to Richard III, there was a later report that Walter Herbert and Rhys opposed Henry Tudor and 'were before him in arms'.

The family history, 'The Life of Sir Rhys ap Thomas', states that Rhys was at hand, with many protestations of loyalty, to meet Henry his 'deer cozen' at the landing beach in Milford Haven. But this episode is imaginary. Rhys was much too sensible, or too calculating, to declare his hand in the opening hours of such a dangerous campaign.

Rather, as soon as news of Henry's landing in Milford Haven reached Rhys, the Welshman started off with some of his forces on a quite independent route to meet Henry Tudor in the upper Severn valley. Rhys's route took him first from Carmarthen along the Tywi valley to Llandovery and thence eastwards to Brecon, three places mentioned in the *Life*. As Rhys advanced, so his pre-arranged reinforcements came in to join him.

Rhys may have deliberately obscured his intentions, perhaps in concert with other Tudor supporters, as part of a deception exercise to confuse Richard III and the King's Welsh agents. With a number of Yorkist castles garrisoned in Wales, necessity surely dictated silence on Rhys's part at this stage of the campaign.

Yet almost certainly there was another reason as well for Rhys's separate route to meet Henry. Rhys wanted to bargain with Henry for suitable rewards in the event of victory. At the same time his scouts were probably in touch with Henry during the stage of their separate marches through Wales. Polydore strongly implies this when he states that two days before their eventual meeting, Henry promised Rhys 'the perpetual lieutenant-ship of Wales so that he would come under his obedience'. Rhys now had an excellent incentive to fight for Henry Tudor's cause.

Once he had reached Brecon, where the potentially hostile forces of the Yorkist Vaughan clan lay to the east, it seems probable that Rhys now pushed northwards over the gentle slopes of the Epynt hills to Builth. The traditional route lies through Llandefaelog and Maes-mynis. At Builth the route lay again northwards along the Wye valley through Rhayader and Llangurig, and so over the watershed into the Severn valley at Llanidloes. This route north of Brecon is conjectural, yet it fits military realities for Rhys's men were on time to meet Henry and other Welsh contingents at Long Mountain (Cefn Digoll) near Welshpool. At no stage along the entire valley route between Builth and Llanidloes does the land rise over 1000 feet.[1]

As we have noted, the family tradition claims that Rhys's force numbered about 2000 horse. In his advance north to join Henry, Rhys may well have adopted the popular military tactic of *La Chevauchée*. This was a fast-moving, flexible deployment of mounted men-at-arms and archers, unencumbered by any large baggage train. This cavalry column, no doubt riding under their leader's black raven standard, thus had a mobility exactly suited to the glens of the Welsh borders.

According to the family *Life*, as his column progressed eastwards and then north, Rhys ordered his prepared warning beacons fired, 'some in one place, some in another on his way to Shrewsbury ... his snowball gathering more and more in the rolling ...'

English ballads of the Tudor period testify to the contemporary impression made by Rhys's part in the Bosworth campaign, even if the size of the column is much exaggerated:

> Then Sir Rhys ap Thomas drawes Wales with him,
> A worthy sight it was to see
> How the Welshmen rose wholly with him
> And stogged them to Shrewsbury ...
> > ('The Rose of England')

> Sir Rhys ap Thomas a knight certain,
> Eight thousand spears brought he ...
> Sir Rhys ap Thomas shall break the array
> For he will fight and never flee ...
> > ('The Ballad of the Lady Bessie')[2]

Some of the risks involved in Rhys's separate advance to join Henry were over once he had reached the upper Severn

[1] See H. N. Jerman, 'A Map of the Routes of Henry Tudor and Rhys ap Thomas through Wales in 1485', *Archaeologia Cambrensis*, 1937.
[2] H. T. Evans, *Wales and the Wars of the Roses*, 1915, pp.224-5.

valley at Llanidloes. From Builth northwards his column was moving through the region of the Mortimer-Yorkist lordships of the Middle March, Maelienydd, Gwerthrynion, Cwmwd Deuddwr, which were held by the King. The Severn marked the boundary of the large lordship of Powis, held by John Grey, Lord Powis, who was believed to be a supporter of Henry's cause. From Llanidloes northwards to Newtown and Welshpool the going was good for a cavalry force.

Rhys now made his rendezvous with Henry Tudor on about 13 August 1485. The probable place of their meeting was at Long Mountain, immediately east of Welshpool. Polydore Vergil tells us that Rhys met Henry 'with a great bande of soldiers, and with assured promysse of loyaltie yielded himself to his protection'.

Although Rhys ap Thomas's contingent was the most important, other Welsh forces joined Henry in this area. These reinforcements came mostly from North Wales. They included the men of Môn and Arfon in north-west Wales under the command of William Gruffydd ap Robin of Cochwillan in the Ogwen valley. There was a contingent from the uplands of Hiraethog under Rhys Fawr ap Maredudd of Plas Iolyn in the upper Conwy valley. Hugh Conway and Richard ap Hywel of Mostyn in Flint came in.

These men from the north brought with them supplies, including fatted oxen and cattle, further evidence of the careful planning behind Henry's advance through Wales. Other gentlemen, not in any particular contingent, but from all parts of Wales and the Marches, made their way individually to join Henry Tudor's combined army on the Welsh border. One of these was David Seisyllt of Alltyrynys in the border lordship of Ewyas Lacy. He was the ancestor of the Cecil family, the famous counsellors of the Tudors.[1]

[1] See A. L. Rowse, 'Alltyrynys and the Cecils', *English Historical Review*, Vol. 74, 1960.

From Long Mountain Henry Tudor's army, about half of which was probably now Welsh, advanced quickly to the vicinity of Shrewsbury twelve miles away. The town gates were closed for a day but on 15 August—perhaps a little later according to some historians—Henry entered Shrewsbury. He had marched the 150 miles from Mill Bay to Shrewsbury in about a week, he had received reinforcements from all over Wales, he had crossed the Severn, and he now stood at the gateway to the English Midlands.

The first part of Henry's campaign had thus ended with the entry into Shrewsbury. All now depended on whether Henry's English allies, and in particular Thomas Lord Stanley and Sir William Stanley, would help him. The Stanleys were by repute opportunistic and moreover Lord Stanley's son, Lord Strange, was held as a hostage by Richard III. Yet there was no alternative for Henry but to press forward for the final confrontation with Richard III.

Bosworth Field, 22 August 1485

Of Sir Rhys ap Thomas's part in the events that culminated with Henry Tudor's victory at Bosworth Field there is, alas, no direct contemporary evidence. The most reliable account of the battle remains that of Polydore Vergil written over twenty years later. But Polydore was a careful historian and had talked to many men who had fought at Bosworth, including almost certainly Henry himself. Polydore's account of the battle has stood the test of time. [1]

Polydore Vergil tells us that from Shrewsbury Henry's army moved eastwards through Newport, Stafford and Tamworth to Atherstone on Watling Street. Henry was here on 20 August. Some English supporters had rallied, but despite his meeting with the Stanleys Henry was still unsure of their intentions. Richard III, meanwhile, had

[1] Polydore Vergil, *Three Books of English History*, 1844, pp. 218-27. The translation of this edition dates from the mid-sixteenth century.

45

received the news of Henry's landing in Wales as early as 11 August, as we have seen, and the King subsequently moved from Nottingham to Leicester. On 21 August the King's army, now fully arrayed, took up position about two miles south of the small town of Market Bosworth to the west of Leicester.

Here the King's forces occupied in line a prominent feature, Ambien Hill, which stood between the villages of Shenton and Sutton Cheney. By the evening of 21 August Henry's army had moved towards the King and stood deployed in the region of Whitemoors plain to the west of Ambien Hill. Battle was now inevitable in the morning.

According to Polydore Vergil, the Tudor army totalled about 5000 men, the forces of Richard III twice that number, while the Stanleys to the north had about 3000 men under the command of Sir William Stanley. But bearing in mind Henry Tudor's reinforcements, perhaps Polydore Vergil understated Henry's strength in order to magnify his subsequent victory. It is a possibility.

The difficulty in assessing Bosworth Field stems not only from the slender source material but from the changes in the landscape since 1485. Then Ambien Hill and its surrounding area was wild, rough grazing land. Since then the country here has been enclosed, drained and cultivated. Many of the details of the fateful encounter must therefore remain conjecture. One recent suggestion is that the real site of the battle is at Dadlington, several miles to the south of Ambien Hill, the traditional battlefield.

However, here we assume that it was on Ambien Hill on the morning of 22 August 1485 that Richard III deployed his army. According to Polydore, Henry Tudor's van was commanded by the veteran Lancastrian, John de Vere, Earl of Oxford, with a force of archers. To the right of the van was Gilbert Talbot, to the left, John Savage of Cheshire.

There was a marsh between the two armies, and Henry decided to keep the bog on his right flank as he ordered Oxford to attack Richard's forces on the hill. Oxford made sure his men kept close to their standards to avoid dispersal. As heavy, but inconclusive, fighting developed between Oxford's men and Richard's own van, led by the Duke of Norfolk, the Stanleys continued to hover to the north of the developing battle. Henry had earlier, but unavailingly, appealed to them for help.

Sensing that the battle was developing into a stalemate, Richard III now decided on a dramatic counter-move that was to cost him his life. Seeing Henry Tudor 'afar off with a small force of soldiers about him' Richard decided to attack his chief adversary. If Henry could be killed, then the battle would be over according to the normal practice of the time. With a small force of troops, the King swept down the slopes of Ambien Hill towards Henry. The claimant's standard-bearer, Sir William Brandon, was struck down; the standard was then picked up by Rhys Fawr ap Maredudd. The fighting was intense.

According to Polydore Vergil, Henry took the shock of Richard's charge with 'great courage' but the situation was clearly desperate. The outcome of Henry's cause was on the knife edge when Sir William Stanley's men came to Henry's aid, sweeping all before them. Richard III was surrounded and killed 'fighting manfully in the thickest press of his enemies'. The King's army disintegrated, and many were killed in the flight that followed. Others threw down their arms, and 'freely submitted themselves to Henry's obeissance'. Richard was dead and Henry had triumphed.

Henry's Acclamation: Rhys is Knighted

The pursuit continued southwards to Stoke Golding, the 'next hill' beyond Ambien. Here, according to Polydore Vergil, Henry was acclaimed King by his jubilant

47

troops who cried, 'God Save King Henry, God Save King Henry!' The acclamation was complete when Lord Stanley found Richard's crown in the spoil of battle and placed it solemnly on Henry's head. Tradition states that the crown was discovered under a thornbush; whatever the historical truth, within a few years a crown in a thornbush had become a badge of the Tudor monarchy.

The battlefield acclamation which initiated the Tudor dynasty was an event of great significance. Acclamation signified that Henry had won the Crown by right of conquest. The God of battles had revealed his will and Divine intervention had given Henry both victory and legitimacy. Conversely, in a rite of degradation, Richard's naked body was thrown over a horse and taken to Leicester for display and burial in the local Greyfriars. The tomb was later destroyed during the Reformation. Bosworth was of course all the more complete a victory because no heir survived Richard III.

Three days after Bosworth Field the new king knighted a number of his associates who had fought with him. These men included Rhys ap Thomas. Subsequently, the sixteenth-century poet Tudur Penllyn was to claim that Rhys Fawr ap Maredudd killed Richard. Another poet, Guto'r Glyn, nearer the event, had no doubt that it was Rhys who had despatched the Boar. The family *Life* of Rhys ap Thomas takes a similar view:

> Our Welch tradition says that Rhys ap Thomas slew Richard manfully fighting with him hand to hand; and we have one strong argument in defence of our tradition, to prove that he was the man who, in all likelihood, had done the deede, for from that time forward, the Earle of Richmond as long as he lived did ever honour him with the title of Father Rhys . . .

Even if this tradition is conjecture, continues the *Life*, Rhys ap Thomas

48

without doubt ... performed some meritoriouse peece of service in that place which made the Earle give him soe honourable an addition to his name.[1]

Of the truth of that particular statement there has never been any doubt.

[1]'The Life of Sir Rhys ap Thomas', p.111.

Chapter IV
Crown Servant: The Bardic Patron

What sort of man was Rhys ap Thomas? The worn, stylised yet impressive tomb-effigy of the knight in St Peter's Church, Carmarthen, conveys a feeling of power and authority but little of personality. Perhaps more true to the man is the bearded, mounted figure, heavily armed with sword and long lance that is found in the traditional representation on the Derwydd bedstead. Here is indisputably the formidable leader of men in battle. We also know that Sir Rhys was a seasoned administrator, a grasping and probably ruthless landlord, and also an accomplished conspirator as the events preceding Bosworth Field demonstrate.

He was medieval in his general outlook and accepted and worked within medieval institutions. He was a loyal son of the Church in the formal sense as his many ecclesiastical bequests show. He held the offices of Justice and Chamberlain of the Principality of South Wales for longer than any other person and probably never questioned the administrative system that had governed Wales since the end of the thirteenth century.

He sprang from the age of chivalry as we can see with some clarity still from the poems of Tudur Aled, Lewis Glyn Cothi and others. He was no ascetic. According to the family *Life*, which relates the information not without a touch of pride, Sir Rhys followed the standard of Venus as well as of Mars, and he acknowledged fourteen natural children, ten by his favourite concubine Gwenllian, sister of the Abbot of Talley.[1] True to the traditions of his family, Sir Rhys became the greatest

[1] 'The Life of Sir Rhys ap Thomas', p.144.

50

bardic patron of his age, dispensing hospitality to his many poets with an almost royal largesse.

In all this complicated, yet not contradictory pattern, two themes above all seem to predominate in Sir Rhys's long career after Bosworth Field. The first is that of Sir Rhys's many-sided role as a great Crown servant of the first two Tudor monarchs. The second theme is that of Sir Rhys's cultivation and enjoyment of bardic favour. The interplay between these two themes, to which we now turn, will help us to understand the whole man.

The New Reign

Following Bosworth Field Sir Rhys ap Thomas quickly became a much-valued Crown servant, filling both administrative and military roles. Rhys's attributes of a regional magnate and of a tested, experienced soldier were of course valuable assets for any king. But Sir Rhys, in addition, seems to have convinced both Henry VII and his son, men whose trust was not easily won, of his complete loyalty to the dynasty. This combination of assets meant that Sir Rhys was to become the virtual Tudor viceroy in West Wales. Sir Rhys's position as a great bardic patron helped to cement this authority for the poets, who saw in him many virtues, were still influential figures in Welsh society.

This amalgam of power and loyalty which characterised Sir Rhys's years as a leading Crown servant was especially fitted to the establishment of an initially insecure reign. Following his acclamation at Bosworth Field, the new King had acted with despatch to establish formally his authority. On 3 September 1485 Henry made his ceremonial entry into the City of London and placed three battle standards borne at Bosworth Field in St Paul's Cathedral.

These banners were the arms of St George which signified Henry's accession to the throne by divine right and by right of conquest; the Red Dragon of Cadwaladr which symbolised his claims to royal Welsh or British descent; a third banner stood for Henry's Lancastrian and Beaufort connections. The Lancastrian greyhound, the Beaufort portcullis, and the Red Dragon of Cadwaladr, all these symbols were now to be blazoned time and again by the new king in a variety of ways to show both his political legitimacy and his personal preoccupation with his complex origins.

After due preparation Henry was then crowned king on 30 October 1485. Soon afterwards Parliament met and confirmed Henry as King without recourse to the legalities of the succession. Henry addressed the Commons and stated that he came to the throne by just hereditary title as well as by the true will of God. As he had promised in exile Henry married Elizabeth of York on 18 January 1486. Through all these ceremonies the succession was confirmed, the opposing factions of York and Lancaster reconciled through marriage, and the blessing of church and state put on Henry's victory at Bosworth.

Yet the new king's hold on the throne must have seemed precarious to contemporaries as he was an unknown, untried monarch. To be sure, Henry had well-qualified advisers in his mother, Lady Margaret Beaufort, the loyal cleric John Morton, who became Chancellor of England in 1486, and his uncle Jasper Tudor amongst others. But Henry had to move very carefully in his search for security, stability, and the firm establishment of the reign. His primary task was to hold the Crown and to pass it on to a legal heir. The problems of Wales were subordinate to these wider preoccupations of the Crown; but Wales also had to be ruled by persons that Henry could trust.

Henry VII's Welsh appointments reflected these priorities. Jasper Tudor, who was created Duke of Bedford, was made Justice of South Wales, restored to the Earldom of Pembroke, and given the important lordships of Glamorgan, Abergavenny and Haverfordwest. Sir Rhys ap Thomas was made Chamberlain of South Wales for life in October 1485 and appointed Steward of the Crown Lordship of Builth. Sir Rhys was also made Constable and Steward of the Lordship of Brecon which was in Crown hands during the minority of Edward, third Duke of Buckingham. In North Wales, Sir William Stanley, who had saved the day at Bosworth, was made Justice of North Wales.

No doubt Sir Rhys, as a supremely realistic practitioner of power, understood the King's concerns, as did Jasper Tudor. Prior to Bosworth, as we have seen, bardic expectations had been pitched at a very high level. The bards had praised Henry Tudor as a deliverer who would bring back the old British line, free Wales from Saxon oppression, and that he would emancipate the Welsh from what Henry himself had called their servitudes. The bards had even sung that a victorious Henry might give the Welsh dominance over the English.

The reality of Henry VII's government in a Wales still divided between March and Principality, and with many English officials still in influential posts, was more mundane than the glorious expectations raised by the bards. Yet the poets were sophisticated men, they knew that the ideal in life always outstripped the reality, so they accepted the new dispensation. Henry had won at Bosworth and nothing could change that. But in any case, early Tudor rule in Wales had some features not seen before in English administration in the country.[1]

In the first place, Henry VII in his own person represented the 'old British line' for as Lewis Glyn Cothi sang in a splendid ode to the new king, he was 'the long bulwark from Brutus' (*'efo yw'r ateg hir o Frutus'*). Moreover Henry made a significant number of Welsh appointments, especially on the level of local adminis-

[1] For a full discussion of this point, see Glanmor Williams, *Recovery, Reorientation and Reformation: Wales c.1415-1642*, 1987, Chapter 10.

tration. In Church affairs, he named during his reign John Morgan and Edward Vaughan as bishops of St Asaph. Thirdly, and late in his reign, Henry issued a number of charters (for sizeable fees) to his subjects in North Wales freeing them from outmoded restrictions.

Henry also made a number of important gestures to show his awareness of his Welsh ancestry and hence his sense of identity with his Welsh subjects. He named his first son Arthur, for example, and he appointed a commission to enquire into his Welsh ancestry. He also encouraged Welshmen at his court. The Welsh dragon features prominently in such early Tudor shrines as King's College Chapel, Cambridge, and in Henry's final resting place in Westminster Abbey. But in most matters of administration and statecraft, efficiency was the new king's watchword. In this complex story of establishing the dynasty, Sir Rhys ap Thomas had a valuable part to play.

Sir Rhys to the Fore

After Bosworth, Sir Rhys was soon called upon to help the King. For the first half of Henry's reign he was troubled by conspiracies and rebellions. The military assistance which Sir Rhys gave the King on a number of occasions must have earned him the sovereign's profound gratitude.

Less than a year after Bosworth in April 1486 there was a rebellion in Wales led by Sir Thomas Vaughan of Tretower who had captured Brecon Castle during Buckingham's revolt in 1483. As we have noted in this connection, Sir Thomas and his kinsmen were veteran Yorkists with a longstanding feud with the Tudors. The rebels tried to take Brecon Castle, and there were also risings at Hay and Tretower. Sir Rhys ap Thomas was called upon to suppress this insurrection. The disturbances must have been relatively serious for 140 soldiers were stationed against the rebels at Brecon Castle for some seven weeks during 1496, at a cost of £48.

During the following year, Henry VII faced what was the most serious military challenge of his reign from a Yorkist pretender, Lambert Simnel. He claimed that he was the Earl of Warwick, the son of Edward IV's dead brother, Clarence. Warwick was in fact locked up in the Tower. A Yorkist force of German mercenaries and Irish levies landed in north-west England but were defeated by Henry's troops at the hard-fought battle of Stoke (near Newark) on 16 June 1487. Sir Rhys ap Thomas commanded 500 horse in the battle which was really the last engagement of the Wars of the Roses.

In a *cywydd* to Sir Rhys's younger brother John of Llandovery—he is sometimes known as 'of Abermarlais'— Lewis Glyn Cothi referred to the civil strife which was now threatening 'tall Harry'. The intention of the rebels was 'to crush the ravens and strike the king', but the counter-intention of the brother of Sir Rhys was 'to crush their skins and hang them'.[1]

At Michaelmas (29 September) 1487 Sir Rhys was appointed Constable of the royal castle of Dinefwr. He probably held this post for the rest of his life. At some time after Bosworth, Sir Rhys was also granted the Duchy of Lancaster castles of Carreg Cennen and Kidwelly. Like Dinefwr the military value of these fortresses had passed away. In any case, Carreg Cennen, as we have seen, had been 'slighted' or partly dismantled after the siege of 1461-62. But the acquisition of these major castles must have enhanced yet again Sir Rhys's authority. Dinefwr Castle shows some evidence of domestic rebuilding in the fifteenth and sixteenth century which may have been the work of Sir Rhys refurbishing the fortress of his ancestor, Lord Rhys.

Sir Rhys took part as one of the captains in Henry VII's expedition against Boulogne in 1492. But significant as was this event in the development of Henry's foreign

[1] *The Poetical Works of Lewis Glyn Cothi*, 1837, *op. cit.*, pp.160-62.

policy, the internal security threat must still have been the King's chief preoccupation.

From about 1491 onwards Henry's reign was distracted by a second Yorkist pretender, Perkin Warbeck. He claimed to be Richard, Duke of York, Edward IV's second son whose death in the Tower in 1483 could not be proved legally. Surprisingly, perhaps, the protracted conspiracy around Perkin Warbeck was supported by Sir William Stanley who was executed for his part in the plot in 1495. After many adventures, Warbeck was eventually captured at Beaulieu Abbey, Hampshire, in September 1497, an event at which Sir Rhys ap Thomas was present with a contingent of Welsh forces.

A few weeks earlier a strong force of rebellious Cornishmen had marched to London. The insurrection was defeated at the Battle of Blackheath (17 June 1497) in which over a thousand rebels were killed. Once again, Sir Rhys played a leading part in an encounter in which Welsh contingents were to the fore. For his valour on the field, Sir Rhys was made knight-banneret. The crushing of this rebellion, combined with the detention of Perkin Warbeck—who was later executed—ended Henry VII's internal security problems and led to the consolidation of the reign.

The Carew Tournament

Although these military actions were central to establishing Henry VII's rule, Sir Rhys was also active in the Crown's attempts to bring better, more efficient government to Wales. Henry of course faced an insuperable task for the country remained divided between the March (with its many independent jurisdictions) and the Principality (with its two centres at Carmarthen and Caernarfon).

To be sure, many of the Marcher lordships were by Henry VII's time in the hands of the Crown including the Duchy of Lancaster lands and the extensive Mortimer

Carew Castle, Pembrokeshire, one of Sir Rhys ap Thomas's favourite residences and scene of the famous tournament of 1507, the last such event held in Britain. (Alan Shepherd Studio)

lordships of the Middle March which were organised under the Earldom of March. These had become Crown properties with the accession of Edward IV in 1461. Other once-independent lordships had escheated to the Crown during the civil wars. Following the execution of Sir William Stanley in 1495, his lordships of Chirk, Holt, and Bromfield and Yale had lapsed to the Crown. In this way the King had become the most important Marcher lord. The problem of corrupt and negligent marcher officials on the local level remained.

Henry VII tried several methods of attempting to bring better government into a clearly obsolete administrative system. He encouraged a system of indentures or legal agreements to promote good government which were made between the Crown and individual Marcher lords. Under these agreements the lords involved were bound to see that their officials closely supervised the processes of

57

law and order. In 1490, for example, an 'Indenture for the Marches' was made between Jasper Tudor as Lord of Glamorgan and other important Marcher lordships. From the same year dates a similar indenture made between Henry VII and 'Sir Rize ap Thomas' as Steward of the Lordships of Builth and Brecon.

Henry VII also attempted to control the age-old problems of Welsh government through a Council of the Marches, a Yorkist innovation first promulgated by Edwards IV in 1471. In 1489 Henry's first son Arthur was made Prince of Wales and given a Council based at Ludlow like its Yorkist predecessor. By 1493 the Council, run of course by officials, had expanded its authority over both Principality and March alike. But Prince Arthur died on 2 April 1502 and although the Council remained in existence its authority waned. The logical conclusion of these efforts by Henry to better order Welsh government lay in the future 'shiring' of Wales by Henry VIII.

As Justice and Chamberlain of the Principality of South Wales, and as Steward of the Lordships of Brecon and Builth, we can see that Sir Rhys was closely involved in Welsh government. Another of his civil duties lay in his role as itinerant justice in the Duchy of Lancaster lordships of South Wales during 1493 and 1504.

These duties would have involved service almost certainly in the Lordship of Kidwelly and perhaps also in the Lordship of Monmouth and the Three Castles (Grosmont, Skenfrith and White) on the south-eastern borders of the March. We should also note that in 1502 Sir Rhys was made Constable of the royal castle of Aberystwyth, an appointment which confirmed yet again his regional authority.

Eventually for all these services, military and civil, Sir Rhys ap Thomas was created a Knight of the Garter on 22 April 1505. The award has been described as 'the ultimate mark of honour favoured by Henry VII'.[1]

[1] S. B. Chrimes, *Henry VII, op. cit.*, p.140.

There was probably little sentiment in these honours and awards given to Sir Rhys by Henry VII. The King might be intensely and even emotionally aware of his Welsh lineage, yet it was competence and reliability that often governed royal appointments in Wales. It may be recalled in this context that the Welsh magnate William Gruffydd of Penrhyn, one of Henry Tudor's supporters, had been reconfirmed as Chamberlain of North Wales after Bosworth. Yet in 1490 Gruffydd had been almost summarily replaced by the English Crown official Sir Richard Pole, who was later appointed Justice of North Wales after the execution of Sir William Stanley in 1495. The Viceregal powers, the honours and the many constableships granted by Henry VII to his warrior subject, Sir Rhys at Thomas, K.G., were probably the just rewards of efficiency and above all loyalty in the service of the Crown.

Some of the wider implications of these awards to Sir Rhys were seen in the great tournament which the knight gave at Carew Castle in April 1507 to celebrate his award of the Garter. Sir Rhys had acquired, probably before Bosworth, and then transformed this medieval fortress on an inlet of Milford Haven into a sophisticated mansion whose ruins still convey something of its former beauty. In particular we can still see over the main porch to the great hall at Carew the coat of arms of Henry VII, Prince Arthur, and Catherine of Aragon, the wife of the Prince (who later married Henry VIII). These armorial emblems were almost certainly added by Sir Rhys. An armorial floor tile in Carew church carries the three ravens emblem of Sir Rhys's family, and is thought to have come from the nearby castle.[1]

The great tournament of April 1507 was the last such gathering in Britain, a celebration from an age that was already passing. It is described in great circumstantial detail in 'The Life of Sir Rhys ap Thomas', detail which

[1] G. W. Spurrell, *The History of Carew*, Carmarthen, 1922, p.81.

suggests an earlier written record. Partly based on this account in the family *Life*, the Pembrokeshire historians of a later time, Richard Fenton and Edward Laws, also described the tournament to good effect.

Altogether, one-thousand persons of rank from all over Wales spent five days in feasting, jousting, hunting and in every form of revelry. There was no quarrelling or ill-feeling. At the head of a great banqueting table, covered in crimson velvet, stood an empty chair for King Henry VII. Over the entrance to Carew Castle was erected, with prescient symbolism of the entire Tudor era, a painting of St George and St David embracing. Such an emblem would have been inconceivable before 1485.

The Derwydd Bedstead, Derwydd house, Llandybïe parish. A portion of the frieze with a mounted figure traditionally representing Sir Rhys ap Thomas, by whom the bed was once owned. (*Transactions of the Carmarthen Antiquarian Society*, Vol. 17 (1923-24), facing p.16) (Photo: Dyfed Archaeological Trust)

Here, then, was surely evidence of the new attitudes of reconciliation not only within Wales, but also of aligned interests between Wales and England brought about by Henry VII and his Welsh followers of which Sir Rhys ap Thomas was but the most prominent. Thus although the forms of the Carew tournament looked backwards to Sir Rhys's own medieval past, the new concord between the Welsh gentry, and between them and the English Crown

> seemed to prefigure the uniting of Wales within itself and the closer relationship with England which was brought about by the legislation of 1536-43. The way for that development had been paved by Henry's ascension to the throne in 1485, which had made much easier the achievement of union half a century later.[1]

There can thus be little doubt that Sir Rhys ap Thomas's career as a Crown servant was of considerable importance in bringing together Wales and England in the prolonged aftermath of Bosworth Field.

The Bardic Patron

Yet for a fuller picture of Sir Rhys in his times we must now mention his activities as a great and generous bardic patron, and try to see in at least an outline what some of those influential contemporaries, the poets, thought of him. The tradition of bardic patronage, of course, came naturally to Sir Rhys. His grandfather, Gruffydd ap Nicholas, was a famous patron, as we have noted, and his father Thomas carried on the tradition. Moreover, both Jasper Tudor and William Herbert, the leading Lancastrian and Yorkist champions in Wales during the Wars of the Roses, were also great and famous patrons, responsible in a large measure for the close relationship between poetry and politics in those turbulent years. The great political leaders of the age were naturally bardic patrons.

[1] Glanmor Williams, *Recovery, Reorientation and Reformation: Wales c.1415-1642, op. cit.*, pp.243-44.

61

Yet in two important respects, the bards saw in Sir Rhys's career distinctive elements which set him apart from the other patrons of the general period. In the first place, the fullness of Sir Rhys's achievements, his military prowess at Bosworth, Stoke and Blackheath, his closeness and blood relationship to Henry VII, his high offices, all tended to bring out the superlatives.

Gruffydd ap Nicholas, it was true, had dominated West Wales for several decades but he had not been given the formal offices held by Sir Rhys. Neither was Gruffydd related to the King in whom many Welshmen, poets and laymen alike, saw the fulfilment of the ancient prophecies of the Welsh destiny.

The praise poem, or the panegyric, had always been one of the chief Welsh poetic forms, presenting its mortal subject in relation to the ideal. In Sir Rhys ap Thomas's case the real and ideal seemed very close indeed for the poets. Tudur Aled (d.c.1525), for example, addressed four *cywyddau* to Sir Rhys. In one of these poems, probably written to celebrate his hero's part in Henry VIII's French campaigns of 1512-13, the writer concluded that the three ravens borne by Sir Rhys were only preceded by God and the King:

> Trecha un draw'n trychu'n y drin
> Tair bran, ond Duw a'r Brenin![1]
>
> ('Superior in advance in the slaughtering battle
> Are the three ravens, next to God and the King!')

A second distinguishing feature in Sir Rhys's life for the poets was the scale of his largesse and the generosity of his patronage. Gruffydd ap Nicholas had welcomed the bards to Newton, and Lewis Glyn Cothi had sung of a tournament at Abermarlais, home of Thomas ap Gruffydd. Jasper Tudor, lord of Pembroke, had been a major bardic patron, but he had of necessity been a

[1] *Gwaith Tudur Aled*, 1926, p.71.

62

fugitive for over twenty years. Even William Herbert, for all the splendour of Raglan Castle, a great centre of bardic patronage, had met his death prematurely after Banbury in 1469.

Sir Rhys ap Thomas's estate, however, surpassed these other bardic patrons. He triumphantly disposed of more castles and mansions than had been held by any Welshman since the Conquest or held indeed by any of the independent princes prior to 1282.

As Justice and Chamberlain of South Wales, Sir Rhys ruled from Carmarthen Castle, the centre of royal power in the region for centuries. In addition, Sir Rhys had been granted the royal castles of Dinefwr and Aberystwyth and the Duchy of Lancaster strongholds of Carreg Cennen and Kidwelly. From the Crown also Sir Rhys held the Lordship of Emlyn with its centre at Newcastle.

Weobley Castle, Gower, one of Sir Rhys ap Thomas's residences, as it might have appeared in 1500. From the reconstruction drawing by D. J. Roberts. *Crown Copyright. Reproduced by permission of the Royal Commission on Ancient and Historical Monuments in Wales.*

63

Neuadd house, on the northern border of the Lordship of Gower with the Black Mountain. Formerly Neuadd Wen, this was the site of Sir Rhys's hunting lodge in the Black Mountain area. (Photo: John Lewis)

Sir Rhys's private possessions included the family mansions at Newton and Abermarlais together with his castles of Carew and of Weobley in Gower. Later in life, in Henry VIII's reign, Sir Rhys was awarded the Lordship of Narberth and made joint Steward (with his son Gruffydd) of the Crown Lordship of Haverfordwest. He controlled both these castles although by this time Haverfordwest Castle was probably beginning to fall into disrepair.

Sir Rhys thus either owned, occupied, or held a dozen historic castles and mansions in West Wales. He also owned, as we have seen, the house of Neuadd Wen on the northern border of the Lordship of Gower with the Black Mountain. This he used as a hunting lodge. We can easily see why the courtly poet Huw Cae Llwyd (d.c.1504), a North Walian who sang the praises of many wealthy families during this period, referred to Sir Rhys in a praise poem as the 'hawk of Deheubarth' ('hebog Deheubarth').[1]

Sir Rhys's Court

The scale of Sir Rhys's patronage was commensurate with this splendid estate. He held court for the poets certainly at Abermarlais, Newton, Kidwelly, Newcastle Emlyn and Carew, the latter castle deep in the Englishry of the Lordship of Pembroke yet a well-known bardic centre in Sir Rhys's time. He may have held court at Weobley and Narberth as well.

Sir Rhys's personal house bard was Rhys Nanmor (*fl.* 1480-1513), who lived for a time at St David's, and who was a *pencerdd*, a member of the highest bardic order. In line with his great patron's loyalties, Rhys Nanmor wrote an elegy on Prince Arthur when he died in 1502 and also an *awdl* (ode) to welcome Henry VIII to the throne in 1509.

In a wider context, Sir Rhys's bardic constituency covered most regions of Wales. A detailed study of the literary traditions of Glamorganshire by Professor Ceri W. Lewis has shown that there were many bardic links between that area and the court of Sir Rhys ap Thomas.

Ieuan Rudd, for example, a Glamorgan bard who flourished in the second half of the fifteenth century, wrote a *cywydd* on the marriage feast of Sir Rhys and his second wife Janet, the daughter of Thomas Mathew of Radyr. It seems very probable that it was this key family tie which henceforth accounted for the very generous patronage which Glamorgan poets received at Sir Rhys's court.

Another of the literary links between Glamorgan and Sir Rhys's court involved the poet Rhisiart ap Rhys Brydydd, or Rhisiart Morgannwg (*fl.* 1480-1520). Rhisiart came from the historic district of Tir Iarll, the area

[1] *Gwaith Huw Cae Llwyd ac Eraill*, 1953, p.90.

covered by Llangynwyd and Bettws parishes in central Glamorgan; he was chided in a *cywydd* by his famous pupil Iorwerth Fynglwyd (d.*c*.1527) for resorting too frequently to the court of Sir Rhys ap Thomas at Kidwelly. But in time, Iorwerth Fynglwyd too became a regular visitor to the court of Sir Rhys, whether at Kidwelly or in Ystrad Tywi at Newton and Abermarlais.

Yet another famous Glamorgan bard who received Sir Rhys's patronage was Lewis Morgannwg (*fl*.1520-65). Thanks to this patronage he was able to meet such important North Wales *penceirddiaid* as Tudur Aled and Lewis Môn (d.*c*.1527) who were also regular visitors to Sir Rhys's court. The friendship between Tudur Aled and Lewis Morgannwg which developed through their contacts at the court of Sir Rhys was especially significant in the latter poet's development.

In this way, Sir Rhys's peripatetic court became a meeting place for poets from all over Wales and 'one of the most important cultural centres in Wales . . . the distinctive cultural *milieu* of Sir Rhys ap Thomas's court was one of the important formative influences in Iorwerth Fynglwyd's bardic career, as it certainly was in Lewis Morgannwg's case'.[1] Both these Glamorgan bards wrote elegies to Sir Rhys after his death in 1525.

Three of the most famous and accomplished poets of the age, Guto'r Glyn (d.*c*.1493), Lewis Glyn Cothi (d.*c*. 1490) and Tudur Aled addressed poems to Sir Rhys ap Thomas. In general, as we have related, poetic expectations had been pitched at a very high note prior to Bosworth Field with Henry Tudor cast as the hero who would restore Welsh dominion over the English.

Yet there was also a worldly element of underlying realism in these bardic hopes. This led to an appreciation of what lay within the bounds of the possible for Henry VII and Sir Rhys ap Thomas once the great victory was won.

[1] Ceri W. Lewis, 'The Literary Tradition of Morgannwg down to the Sixteenth Century', in *Glamorgan County History*, Vol. III, 1971, p.512.

66

But there can be little doubt that in any case the poets genuinely admired Sir Rhys and very little prompting was needed to praise his achievements in these eulogies. After all, like Henry VII, Sir Rhys was a winner.

Thus in his *cywydd* to 'Sir Rhys of Abermarlais' Guto'r Glyn invoked Sir Rhys's contribution to Henry's triumph at Bosworth. First the poet asserted his general admiration of Sir Rhys:

> Syr Rhys, ni welais ŵr gwell
> Na'i gystal yn ei gastell

('I have not seen in his Castle a nobler man than Sir Rhys or even his equal.')

Then Guto'r Glyn praised the specific part played at Bosworth by Sir Rhys:

> Brain Urien a'i brynarodd.
> Cwncweriodd y King Harri
> Y maes, drwy nerth ein meistr ni.
> Lladd y baedd, eilliodd ei benn . . . [1]

> ('The ravens of Urien prepared the victory.
> King Henry conquered the field
> through the strength of our master [Sir Rhys].
> Killed the Boar, destroyed his head . . .')

Whatever the historical truth, for Guto'r Glyn it was Sir Rhys who had slain the arch-enemy on the battlefield.

A different theme was chosen in a striking ode by Lewis Glyn Cothi in praise of Sir Rhys ap Thomas and Jasper Tudor. The poet stressed that after Bosworth the ancient ruling house of Britain had returned in the persons of Henry Tudor, Jasper Tudor and Sir Rhys. All three were descended from Goronwy and Gruffydd, children of Ednyfed Fychan and Gwenllian, descendants of Rhodri the Great and Tewdwr Mawr:

[1] *Gwaith Guto'r Glyn*, 1939, pp.263-64.

Yr ynys hon a rannwyd
I wŷr annwyl o'r unwaed . . .
Goronwy, Gruffydd, gŵyr o anian,—plaid
Plant Ednyfed Fychan,
A'u mam oedd hi Gwenllian,
Ŵyr Tewdwr . . .
Eisilltydd Rhodri Mawr . . . [1]

('The island is divided
between men of the same blood . . .
Goronwy, Gruffydd, men of quality,
of the party of the children of Ednyfed Fychan
And their mother was that Gwenllian,
descendant of Tewdwr . . .
Progeny of Rhodri the Great . . .')

Lewis also sang that the stars as well as the ancient Welsh prophets had long ago assigned the kingdom to the men of Gwynedd. Sir Rhys, a 'kinsman of the king', a 'golden knight' was now part of this inheritance. Lewis Glyn Cothi had been the veteran laureate of the House of Dinefwr for three generations, but even he had probably never praised the ravens with such fervour as in this poem to Sir Rhys.

In his poems dedicated to Sir Rhys, the North Walian Tudur Aled rang the changes on the basic poetic themes, which 'fab Urien', the son of Urien, as he called him, seemed to inspire in the poets. The military prowess of their great patron, the blood link with the old Welsh rulers and their successors, the Tudors, Sir Rhys's great estates and his many castles, his chivalric Arthurian qualities, all these images appear in the poems of Tudur Aled, the most famous contemporary poet.

In one of these striking praise-poems to his hero, Tudur Aled calls Sir Rhys the 'pinnacle of all Wales' (pinagl holl Cymru').[2]

Yet one passage in particular seems to distil these themes, and moreover provides the poet's personal view

[1] The Poetical Works of Lewis Glyn Cothi, 1837, op.cit., p.164.
[2] Gwaith Tudur Aled, 1926, p.38.

of Sir Rhys towards the end of his life. These are the concluding lines from Tudur Aled's poem to Sir Rhys, 'D'enw Yn Fyw No Dyn yn Fyw', 'Your Name Greater Than Any Man Living':

> Caterwen, capten y cwbl,
> Caerfyrddin, caerau curddwbl;
> Drwys a gyrraedd dros Gaeryw,
> D'enw yn fwy no dyn yn fyw . . .
> Dwg enw yn uwch dug na neb,
> Drych henaint ar ych wyneb.[1]

> ('Spreading oak-tree, Captain of all,
> Carmarthen, two golden fortresses;
> Door which extends over Carew
> Your name greater than any man living . .
> Bearing a name higher than is borne by anyone
> Old age mirrored in your face.')

As these lines illustrate, there was probably a genuine affection between Sir Rhys and Tudur Aled quite apart from the formal relationship between poet and patron. Yet there was an historic paradox in all this splendid patronage for Sir Rhys presided over what was the last great flowering of the bardic culture. With the death of Tudur Aled at about the same time as Sir Rhys, and that of Lewis Morgannwg a generation later, the classical bardic order went into a decline in the face of profound social changes in Wales, changes which neither Sir Rhys nor his many bards could have foreseen.

Last Campaigns

After Henry VII's death on 21 April 1509 'Father Rhys' continued in royal favour with the new king. Henry VIII quickly confirmed Sir Rhys in office and was soon to draw on his military experience. Unlike Henry VII who relied mostly on Sir Rhys's military skills in the internal consolidation of his reign, the new king called for support

[1] *Gwaith Tudur Aled*, 1926, p.75.

69

in his French campaigns. Despite all the uncertainties of Henry VII's early reign, the succession had passed naturally and without challenge to his son, and Henry VIII was free—for the first half of his reign—to devote his attention to foreign matters and England's place in the concert of Europe.

In 1512 Sir Rhys and his son, Sir Gruffydd, together with a retinue of 500 men, accompanied Henry VIII on a French expedition. Sir Rhys distinguished himself at the siege of Guienne, but Sir Gruffydd managed to lose several guns during the campaign. Sir Rhys returned to Flanders in 1513, but without his son, and excelled again at the siege of Thérouanne. These two successive expeditions were Sir Rhys's last military campaigns, an impressive performance for a man of over sixty.

Probably as a reward for these military services, Sir Rhys continued to accumulate from the Crown territorial awards and other offices in West Wales. In June 1515 he was given the Lordship of Narberth and one-third of the Lordship of St Clears. Two years later in June 1517 Sir Rhys and his son Sir Gruffydd were jointly granted for life the offices of Steward, Chancellor and Receiver of the Lordship of Haverfordwest.

As he approached his seventieth year, Sir Rhys probably assumed that the succession of his enormous estates was safe enough in the hands of his son Sir Gruffydd. He was primarily a courtier, and not a soldier, and his early career was involved with Prince Arthur. Gruffydd had attended Arthur's wedding with Catherine of Aragon in November 1501 and was then made a Knight of the Bath. Following the Prince's death in April 1502, Sir Gruffydd had borne the Prince's arms at the funeral in Worcester Cathedral.

Sir Gruffydd's career as a courtier had continued after Prince Arthur's death and from 1513-15 he was a member of the royal household. With his father he attended the Field of the Cloth of Gold, Henry VIII's celebrated meeting with the German Emperor in 1520. Sir Gruffydd was also associated with his father in local government in Wales and in 1514 he was mayor of Kidwelly. He also rented some Crown estates in Cardiganshire.[1]

Whatever Sir Rhys's hopes for the succession involving his son they were ended by Sir Gruffydd's premature death in 1521. Like Prince Arthur he was buried in Worcester Cathedral where an impressive tomb survives. With Sir Gruffydd's death, Sir Rhys's heir now became his grandson, the young Rhys ap Gruffydd. He was the son of Sir Gruffydd and his wife Catherine St John. Had Sir Gruffydd lived, the eventual disposition of Sir Rhys's estates might well have taken a different course.

The Paradox of Government

Finally, we must ask in view of Sir Rhys's long service as a Crown official, what was his contribution to Tudor government in West Wales? Such an assessment is not easy. The great problem of medieval government in Wales and the Marches was the multiple division of authority exacerbated in the fifteenth century by private interest, internal war and rebellion.

Tudor rule in Wales during Sir Rhys's lifetime had tried, not without partial success, to remedy these anarchic tendencies. In West Wales in particular Sir Rhys ap Thomas's great authority, exercised over four decades, and reflected in bardic acclaim, helped to convince the populace that Tudor rule was the natural order. The very continuity of office which Sir Rhys brought to his duties contrasted tellingly with the tensions and upheavals of the forty years preceding Bosworth Field in 1485. There was thus a recovery of royal authority in West Wales during Sir Rhys's time in office.

Yet there was an important paradox in early Tudor rule in Wales for the underlying problems of Welsh government remained. Chief amongst these was the

[1] For further details of Sir Gruffydd's career, see R. A. Griffiths, *The Principality of Wales in the Later Middle Ages*, 1972, *op.cit.*, pp.190-91.

problem of separate jurisdictions. This meant that offenders, as in the past, could escape from lordship to lordship, or from lordship to Principality and *vice versa.* Escaping lawbreakers could put themselves under a Marcher lord's protection by paying an avowry fine, or the *arddel.* Sometimes it was easier to bribe the appropriate official to escape justice. Intimidation was in any case very common. Another option for the malefactor was to escape from either March or Principality to the entirely separate jurisdiction of England.

A government report of 1533 identified three main causes of disorder in Wales which would have been present during Sir Rhys's time. These were that murder and cattle stealing went unpunished, that juries would not convict, and thirdly the prevalence of the illegal fine or exaction known as the *commortha.* Thus while there was some improvement in public order in Wales under Henry VII, 'within a decade of Henry VIII's accession the King's ministers believed that the forces of disorder in Wales were becoming more difficult to check and that view was probably well founded . . .'[1]

That these forces of disorder were prevalent in West Wales, and involved officialdom at the highest level, may be seen in the lengthy Bill of Complaint presented by Sir Clement West to the Court of Requests in 1520. Sir Clement had been appointed Head of the Commandery of the Knights of St John at Slebech in 1513. This was the famous foundation of the Knights Hospitallers on the eastern Cleddau river. Sir Clement deposed that he had cause for complaint against Sir Rhys ap Thomas and his son Gruffydd for having unlawfully cut down timber belonging to the Knights of St John, for extorting considerable sums of money from the Order's tenants, and that Sir Rhys's men had broken into Sir Clement's house.[2]

[1] *Glamorgan County History,* Vol. III, 1971, *op.cit.,* pp.565, 561.
[2] Francis Jones, 'Sir Rhys ap Thomas and the Knights of St John', *The Carmarthen Antiquary,* Vol. 2,1945-57, p.70-74.

There seems little reason to doubt Sir Clement's allegations. Such incidents help to explain why the governmental system in Wales, and which Sir Rhys represented in the West, was swept away barely a decade or so after his death in 1525. Profound religious changes were also decreed in this period by Henry VIII as the king's attention turned to domestic and dynastic matters after about 1527. Nor did the House of Dinefwr escape the storm. In less than a decade after Sir Rhys's death his heir was destroyed and his very large estates confiscated by the Crown. Sir Rhys ap Thomas was destined to be the last great Welshman of the Middle Ages.

Chapter V
Death at the Greyfriars

In early 1525 the 'spreading oak-tree' at last fell when Sir Rhys ap Thomas came to die at the Carmarthen Greyfriars. It was here on 3 February that Sir Rhys made his will in which he asked that he be buried in the chancel of the Friary Church 'there as my mother lyeth and whensoever it pleaseth God to call my wife my will is that she be buried with me ...'

Sir Rhys left twenty pounds to the Friars and another five pounds 'for a chantry there to fynd two priests to pray for me and my wife for ever ...' This latter bequest involved the creation of a small chapel where masses would be sung for Sir Rhys's soul.

The Friary Church, although not large, contained many treasures and included a steeple containing a clock and two bells. Today nothing remains above ground although recent excavation has revealed extensive foundations.

There were buried here many of the later medieval gentry of West Wales including some members of Sir Rhys's family. These included Gruffydd ap Nicholas, Sir Rhys's mother, Elizabeth of Abermarlais, and Sir Rhys's son, Sir Gruffydd. One of Sir Rhys's ancestors, on his mother's side, who lay buried at the Greyfriars was the famous soldier and Crown servant Sir Rhys ap Gruffydd (d.1356). It was to the Friary Church that Bishop William Barlow, the first Reformation bishop of St David's (1536-48), urged the removal of his own cathedral church.

Sir Rhys died on 9 February 1525 and his body lay in state in the Greyfriars until he was buried in the choir or chancel on 24 February.

Amongst many of Sir Rhys's ecclesiastical bequests in West Wales were the following:

74

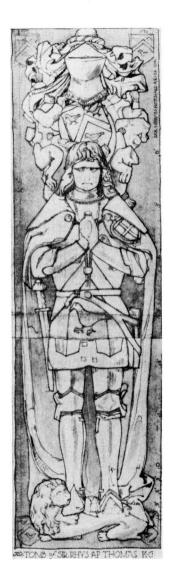

The tomb-effigy of Sir Rhys ap Thomas in St Peter's Church, Carmarthen. Originally erected at the Greyfriars, the tomb was moved to St Peter's after the Dissolution of the Friary in 1538. From the drawing by Ivor Merfyn Pritchard. (RCAHM, *Carmarthenshire Inventory*, 1917, p.253.) *Crown Copyright. Reproduced by permission of the Royal Commission on Ancient and Historical Monuments in Wales.*

To the Cathedral Church of St. David's	£20
To St. John's Priory Chapel, Carmarthen	£6 13s 4d
To the Rood Church (St. Mary's) of Carmarthen, a vestment worth	40s
To St. Barbara's Chapel, Carmarthen, a vestment worth	40s
To St. Catherine's Chapel, Carmarthen, a vestment worth	40s
To the Church of Llandyfeisant, by Newton, a vestment worth	40s
To the Lady Chapel at the Bridge End of Cothi, a vestment worth	40s
A Cross of Silver to the Parish Church of Carew	

In addition, Sir Rhys willed that his wife Janet, who died in 1535, was to receive one-third of the lands and lordships which he had enjoyed during her lifetime. She was also to receive all Sir Rhys's properties in Old and New Carmarthen. After other bequests, the rest of Sir Rhys's very considerable estates and lordships were left to Sir Rhys's grandson, Rhys ap Gruffydd. It was he who now became Sir Rhys ap Thomas's heir.[1]

Two famous bards, Iorwerth Fynglwyd and Lewis Morgannwg, who had shared Sir Rhys's patronage, wrote elegies to him. Iorwerth Fynglwyd sang eloquently:

> Cawn yn unair can hynys,
> Can sir, yn cwyno Syr Rhys:
> Canu a wnawn cwyn anianol,
> Canwae ni'n cwyno'n ei ôl.
> Cymro brig Cymru o'i bron,
> Cwyn holl Loegr cannwyll llygion . . . [2]

> ('A hundred islands are as one voice,
> A hundred shires to mourn Sir Rhys
> We shall sing a deep lament,
> A hundred woes to us who mourn after him.
> A Welshman, leader of Wales, nursed on her breast,
> The whole of England mourns with bright candles . . .')

[1] For an abstract of Sir Rhys's will, see David Jones, 'Sir Rhys ap Thomas', *Archaeologia Cambrensis*, 1892, pp.90-91.
[2] *Gwaith Iorwerth Fynglwyd*, 1975, p.45.

Tudur Aled wrote no elegy to Sir Rhys. Bardic tradition asserts that he too died at the Greyfriars at about the same time as Sir Rhys, perhaps a little later, and that the poet was buried in the Friary graveyard, clad in the habit of a grey friar.

But the names of famous poet and great patron continued to be linked for in an elegy to Tudur Aled his fellow bard Lewis Morgannwg wrote of Sir Rhys:

> Nid oes gwin, dywysog ynys,
> Nid oes rodd, wedi Sir Rhys!
> Bwrw un urddol . . .[1]
>
> ('There is no wine, prince of the island,
> There is no gift after Sir Rhys!
> A noble one has been smitten . . .)

Conclusion

In death as in life Sir Rhys ap Thomas remained associated with the Tudors, for also buried in the choir of the Carmarthen Greyfriars was his distant kinsman, Edmund Taylor, Earl of Richmond, father of Henry VII. This was only appropriate for Sir Rhys's life and career was inseparably linked with the first two Tudor monarchs. How, then, may we assess Sir Rhys's career as a whole?

In the first place, there can be little doubt that Rhys ap Thomas's assistance to Henry of Richmond in August 1485 was probably decisive. Without Rhys's help, the march to Bosworth could hardly have taken place. We must remember that Rhys ap Thomas's 'great bande of soldiers' (Polydore Vergil) which joined Henry Tudor's army near Long Mountain, and which significantly augmented his force, could just as easily have intercepted the Tudor army in West Wales or further north in the Cambrian mountains. According to S. B. Chrimes, Henry's latest and perhaps most authoritative biographer, 'he

---

[1] *Gwaith Tudur Aled*, 1926, p.xliv.

77

owed much, perhaps everything, in the final progress towards Bosworth, to either Welsh support, or at least Welsh abstention from opposition in the critical days of August 1485'.[1]

The Raven thus played an indispensable military role in the events that culminated at Bosworth Field. Neither must we forget the important military support given by Sir Rhys to Henry VII at the battles of Stoke (1487) and Blackheath (1497). These were encounters which led to the final consolidation of the reign which was far being preordained by Henry's victory at Bosworth. At last, with the suppression of the rebellion of 1497, the disturbances and civil wars of the fifteenth century were ended.

In a more purely Welsh context it should be stressed, secondly, that Sir Rhys ap Thomas's career marked the undisputed emergence of a Welsh landed class in the later middle ages. By his ability and willpower, by the determined application of his resources, and by his loyalty to Henry VII and his son, Rhys was able to dominate the society of West Wales for some forty years after Bosworth.

The House of Dinefwr in the person of Rhys had thus attained great, probably unprecedented power for a native Welsh magnate family after the Conquest. Of course, unlike the power exercised by Gruffydd ap Nicholas, Rhys deployed his authority not in defiance of the Crown but in support of the King. Yet the seventeenth-century English historian, Thomas Fuller, was surely correct when he wrote that although Rhys ap Thomas 'was never more than a knight, he was little less than a prince in his native country' (*Worthies*, 1662).

This consideration leads us to a third, related, aspect of Sir Rhys's life and career. It appears probable that Sir Rhys's career showed to his colleagues of the Welsh gentry that the course of self-interest and self-advancement lay in unity and common purpose; to be sure, it took several generations for the often endemic violence of Welsh life in

[1] S. B. Chrimes, *Henry VII, op.cit.*, p.3.

78

the later middle ages to yield to the dictates of the Tudor peace. But Sir Rhys's career, characterised by both bardic acclaim and very real royal patronage, was an example which helped to unify Wales after the unrest of the fifteenth century. The harmony which prevailed at Sir Rhys's great tournament at Carew Castle had more than symbolic value.

Above all, Sir Rhys ap Thomas's career illustrated the decisive alignment of interests between the Welsh gentry an the English Crown as represented by the Tudors. A psychological union between Wales and the Crown had occurred with Bosworth Field as we can see in the bardic eulogies to Sir Rhys. Under Henry VIII, the Acts of Union of 1536 and 1543 gave statutory recognition to the Welsh gentry as rulers of their own society. But Sir Rhys's career, in its military, administrative, and social aspects, had already presaged the legislative Union of Wales and England with its formal recognition of the leading role of the Welsh gentry in governing Wales.

In short, Sir Rhys ap Thomas's life pointed the way forward for an entire Welsh landed class which was to come into its own after the Act of Union of 1536. Sir Rhys was born and lived in one age, but by his interests, his actions and his loyalties he anticipated the next age, one which sees the foundations laid of modern Wales. Future scholarship will almost certainly reveal further information about Sir Rhys, one of the most interesting and significant of Welshmen.

Epilogue
The Fall of the House of Dinefwr

The death of Sir Rhys ap Thomas in 1525 marked the virtual end of the middle ages in Wales. But for a few years the old order remained unchanged. When a herald from the College of Arms, William Fellow, visited the Church of the Carmarthen Greyfriars in 1530 he noted that 'before thymage of St Fraunces lyeth buried in a tombe of allabastre, Gryffyth Nycolas esquier' and that 'in the quyer on the northside a lytle from the high aulter lyeth buried in a goodly tombe Sir Ryce ap Thomas . . .'

As we have noted Sir Rhys's far-flung estates had descended to his young grandson, Rhys ap Gruffydd, who was aged about seventeen in 1525. But the two most important Crown offices held by Sir Rhys ap Thomas, those of Justice and Chamberlain of South Wales, were granted by Henry VIII to Walter Devereux, Lord Ferrers.

Rhys ap Gruffydd's probable resentment of these grants to Ferrers, compounded by his youth and perhaps by the influence of his strong-willed wife, Lady Catherine Howard, was now to bring ruin to the House of Dinefwr and Rhys's own execution.

The events are shadowy but in the summer of June 1529 a quarrel erupted between Ferrers and the popular Rhys and Gruffydd over billeting arrangements for their retainers in Carmarthen.[1] Rhys was arrested and imprisoned in Carmarthen Castle, an event which led to a riot probably instigated by Rhys's wife. Rhys was released on bail but the authorities were alarmed at what was termed insurrection. Later that year Rhys ap Gruffydd was summoned before the Court of the Star Chamber, a

[1]For a full account of the Rhys ap Gruffydd episode, see W. Llewelyn Williams, A Welsh Insurrection', *Y Cymmrodor*, Vol. 16, 1903.

hearing which unavailingly ended with an injunction to Rhys and Ferrers to make peace with each other. Then, in October 1530, Rhys ap Gruffydd was rearrested, and lodged in the Tower until June 1531. He was then released briefly, but eventually tried before the Court of the King's Bench in September and found guilty of having conspired and plotted to depose Henry VIII and replace him by James V of Scotland. Rhys was then executed for treason on 4 December 1531.

One of the charges against Rhys was that he had encouraged seditious prophecies that the Ravens, together with the King of Scotland would conquer England. He was also accused of having adopted the name of FitzUrien so that 'he might more worthily obtain the principality of Wales, which was the mark he assigned after the conquest'. Evidently, the potent, emotional raven symbols so beloved by the bards possessed a lethal quality for their hapless bearer when confronted with the suspicions of Tudor statecraft. It was also believed by some contemporaries that another reason for Rhys's downfall was that he had been Critical of Anne Boleyn and her friendship with the King.

Although the precise reasons for the elimination of Rhys ap Gruffydd may never be known, the general context of early Tudor policy make it clear that his ancestry, his regional power, and not least the aura of political prophecy which surrounded the House of Dinefwr put Rhys in great jeopardy once the apprehensions of the Crown were aroused.

Both Henry VII and his son consciously acted to restrict the power of the feudal nobility. The early Tudor kings were concerned, not without reason, that such persons might lead armed insurrections against the Crown. In 1521 Edward Stafford, Third Duke of Buckingham, the last of the great Welsh marcher lords, had gone to the block for arousing such fears in Henry VIII. The riots in Carmarthen in 1529, and the prophecies or dreams which

Rhys ap Gruffydd may have uttered, probably led the King, concerned with good government in Wales, and contemplating the break with Rome, to cut down the House of Dinefwr. Prolonged disorder in Wales at this critical stage of the reign would have been intolerable. The removal of Rhys ap Gruffydd would in any case have had a profound deterrent effect on his followers, received as it no doubt was with terror.

Following the destruction of Rhys ap Gruffydd his extensive estates were made forefeit to the Crown by Act of Attainder. A far-reaching redistribution of the lands once inherited and acquired by Sir Rhys ap Thomas now took place.

It is illustrative of Tudor policy that in April 1532 Hugh Vaughan, Groom of the Chamber and Forester of Kidwelly, was appointed to be Keeper and Receiver of the forfeited lands in Kidwelly, Carnwyllion and Iscennen. Hugh Vaughan's son, John, also obtained Crown leases of the confiscated lands in Kidwelly, Iscennen, St Clears and Carmarthen Town. These grants were the foundations on which the politically reliable Vaughans of Golden Grove were to build their own extensive estates.

Sir Rhys ap Thomas's considerable properties in the Lordship of Gower, comprising Landimore, Weobley Castle, Cae Gurwen and Neuadd Wen, were not included in these grants to the Vaughans. Instead these estates were eventually sold by Elizabeth I in 1560 to a loyal executant of Tudor policy, William Herbert (d.1570), First Earl of Pembroke (of the second creation).[1]

In addition, following the Act of Attainder, a large number of the confiscated properties of Rhys ap Gruffydd were later sold on a commercial basis by the Crown. These properties included many separate holdings in the commote of Hirfryn (Cantref Bychan) and in Catheiniog, Maenordeilo, Mallaen and in the forest of Glyncothi

[1] David Rees, 'Neuadd Wen: Changing Patterns of Tenure', in H. James (ed.), *Sir Gâr: Studies in Carmarthenshire History*, 1991.

(Cantref Mawr). Many of these properties in north Carmarthenthshire, and which of course had once been owned by Sir Rhys ap Thomas, were sold by Crown officials to speculators such as Harry Campion, a London merchant.[1]

In time Sir Rhys ap Thomas's descendants recovered some of his Carmarthenshire estates, including Dinefwr and Newton, but the remainder of the forfeited lands in West Wales were disposed of by the Crown.

Within a few years of Rhys ap Gruffydd's execution, fundamental changes in the secular and ecclesiastical affairs of Wales were decreed by the Crown. The Act of Union of 1536 swept away the royal Principality of Wales and also the Marcher Lordships, 'shired' Wales on the English pattern, and extended English law, civil and criminal, throughout Wales. Wales was now incorporated within the English realm. A subsequent (and comprehensive) Act of 1543 laid down in great detail the new administrative and judicial system in Wales.

In ecclesiastical affairs, a series of Acts passed between 1529 and 1534 transferred papal authority in England and Wales to the Crown and made Henry VIII supreme head of the church. The King now proceeded to seize the church assets. Most of the Welsh monasteries were dissolved in 1536. On 30 August 1538, the instrument of surrender of the Carmarthen Greyfriars to the Crown was signed. The inventory noted that in the Friary church was 'a goodly tumbe for Sir Ryse ap Thomas, with a grate of yron abowthe him, a stremar banner of hys arms with his cote armour and helmit . . .'

Shortly afterwards, the tomb of Henry VIII's grand-father, Edmund Tudor, was taken from the Greyfriars to St. David's Cathedral, where it remains. At the same time, Sir Rhys's tomb was transferred to St. Peter's Church, Carmarthen. The tomb was placed in the north

[1]Williams, Rhys Davys, 'Forfeited Lands of Rhys ap Gruffydd', in *Carmarthen Antiquary*, Vol. V, 1964-69, pp.46-48.

The tomb of Sir Rhys ap Thomas and his second wife, Janet, in St Peter's Church, Carmarthen. A general view from the east of the Church. (Photo: Dyfed Archaeological Trust)

84

side of the chancel, where it remained until 1865 when it was moved to the aisle and restored.

But the effigy of Sir Rhys, dressed in armour, still lies on the great covering slab. At his side is his sword, and above his head the armorial ravens of his house and his helmet. Next to him lies the effigy of his second wife, Janet.

Not long after the transfer of this tomb it was recorded during 1543 that the buildings of the Greyfriars were 'in contynnual ruyne and decaie'. By this time a new order in church and state was slowly arising in Wales, an order which by his role in the creation of the Tudor dynasty Rhys ap Thomas had done more than any other Welshman to bring about.

SIR RHYS AP THOMAS'S MANOR HOUSE AT NEWTON

APPENDIX

Following the execution of Rhys ap Gruffydd in December 1531 (Epilogue, above), Parliament passed an Act of Attainder in January 1532 through which Rhys's estates and possessions were confiscated by the Crown. A subsequent survey of the Manor of Newton, *circa* 1532, gave details of the family mansion. The Manor had probably changed very little since the time of Sir Rhys ap Thomas who kept a residence there.

According to the Survey, the Manor of Newton stood within the town of Newton and was said to have 'but small commodities apertaining to it'. A flight of twelve steps led to a hall thirty three-feet long, and twenty feet broad, paved with Flanders tiles and roofed with slate. At the west end of the hall was a chamber also tiled and 'selyd with borde', and at the north end of this room was a little chamber twelve feet square. There were also two inner rooms and a study.

At the east end of the hall was a chamber paved with tiles, under which was a low chamber. On the south side of the hall was a stone tower which contained a low, vaulted chamber with a chapel above, paved with Flanders tiles. Also on the south side of the hall was a kitchen, a larder and a buttery. There was also a vaulted wine cellar underneath the main hall.

At the entrance to the hall on the north side there was a low chamber known as the porter's lodge. There was also a large bakehouse and a brewhouse, with a chamber above which held corn.

Outside the Manor was a stable and a loft covered with slate, and a barn covered with straw and in decay. Also a 'stable decaied' with the walls standing and measuring in length 33 feet and 25 feet broad. Another decayed stable was 23 feet long 'with the timber of the same standing'.

(Sources: *Carmarthenshire Inventory*, 1917, p.110; PRO E315/151 in *West Wales Historical Records*, Vol. II, 1912, pp. 118-19.

Chrimes, S. B., *Henry VII*, Eyre Methuen, London, 1972.

Evans, Howell T., *Wales and the Wars of the Roses*, Cambridge University Press, 1915.

Griffiths, Ralph A., 'Gruffydd ap Nicholas and the Rise of the House of Dinefwr', *National Library of Wales Journal*, Vol. 13, No. 2, 1964.

Griffiths, Ralph A., 'Gruffydd ap Nicholas and the Fall of the House of Lancaster,' *Welsh History Review*, Vol. 2, No. 3, 1965.

Griffiths, Ralph A., *The Principality of Wales in the Later Middle Ages:* I: *South Wales 1277-1536*, University of Wales Press, Cardiff, 1972.

Griffiths, Ralph A., (and Roger S. Thomas). *The Making of the Tudor Dynasty*, Alan Sutton, Gloucester, 1985.

Harries, Leslie, *Gwaith Huw Cae Llwyd ac Eraill*, University of Wales Press, Cardiff, 1953.

James, Heather (Ed.), *Sir Gar: Studies in Carmarthenshire History: Essays in Memory of W. H. Morris and M. C. S. Evans*, Carmarthenshire Antiquarian Society, 1991.

James Terrence, *Carmarthen: An Archaeological and Topographical Survey*, Dyfed Archaeological Trust and Carmarthenshire Antiquarian Society, 1980.

Jarman, A. O. H. & Hughes, G. R., *A Guide to Welsh Literature*, Vol. 2, Christopher Davies, Swansea, 1979.

Jarman, H. N., 'A Map of the Routes of Henry Tudor and Rhys ap Thomas Through Wales in 1485', *Archaeologia Cambrensis*, 1937.

Jones, David, 'Sir Rhys ap Thomas', *Arch. Camb.*, 1892.

Jones, E. D., 'Wales in Fifteenth Century Politics', in *Wales Through the Ages*, Vol. 1, Christopher Davies, Swansea, 1975 ed.

Jones, E. D., (Ed.), *Lewes Glyn Cothi (Detholiad)*, University of Wales Press, Cardiff, 1984.

Jones, E. D., *Beirdd y Bymthegfed Ganrif a'u Cefndir*, Centre for Advanced Welsh and Celtic Studies, Aberystwyth, 1984.

Jones, Francis, 'Sir Rhys ap Thomas', *Trans. Carmarthenshire Antiquarian Society*, Vol. 29, 1939.

Jones, Francis, 'Sir Rhys ap Thomas and the Knights of St. John', *The Carmarthen Antiquary*, Vol. 2, 1945-57.

Jones, Francis, 'The Grey Friars of Carmarthen', *The Carmarthen Historian*, Vol. 3, 1966.

Jones, Francis, 'Abermarlais', *Arch. Camb.*, 1967.

Jones, J. & Davies, W. (Eds.), *The Poetical Works of Lewis Glyn Cothi*, Oxford, 1837.

87

Jones, T. Gwynn (Ed.), *Gwaith Tudur Aled*, University of Wales Press, Cardiff, 1926.

Lewis, Ceri W., 'The Literary Tradition of Morgannwg down to the Sixteenth Century', in T. B. Pugh (ed.), *Glamorgan County History:* Vol. III: *The Middle Ages*, 1971.

'The Life of Sir Rhys ap Thomas' ... 'A short view of the long life of the ever-wise, valiant, and fortunate commander, Rhys ap Thomas, Knight, Constable Lieutenant of Brecknock', *Cambrian Register*, Vol. 1, 1795, pp. 49-144.

Lloyd, H. W., 'Sir Rhys ap Thomas and his family', *Arch. Camb.*, 1878.

Lloyd, Sir J. E., *A History of Carmarthenshire*, Vol. I, Cardiff, 1935.

Lloyd, Sir J. E., 'Sir Rhys ap Thomas', in *Dictionary of National Biography*, London, Vol. 48, 1896.

Lloyd, J. M., 'The Rise and Fall of the House of Dinefwr (the Rhys Family) 1430-1530', M.A. Dissertation, University of Wales, 1963.

Meyrick, Sir S. R., *The Heraldic Visitations of Lewis Dwnn*, 1846.

Rees, David, *The Son of Prophecy: Henry Tudor's Road to Bosworth*, Black Raven Press, London, 1985.

Rees, David, 'Neuadd Wen: Changing Patterns of Tenure', in Heather James (Ed.), *Sir Gâr: Studies in Carmarthenshire History*, 1991.

Rees, Sir J. F., 'Sir Rhys ap Thomas', *Dictionary of Welsh Biography*, Hon. Society of Cymmrodorion, 1959.

Richards, W. Leslie (Ed.), *Gwaith Dafydd Llwyd o Fathafarn*, University of Wales Press, Cardiff, 1964.

Ross, Charles, *The Wars of the Roses*, Eyre Methuen, London, 1976.

Ross Charles, *Richard III*, Eyre Methuen, 1981.

Rowlands, E. I. (Ed.), *Gwaith Iorwerth Fynglwyd*, University of Wales Press, Cardiff, 1975.

Rowse, A. L., *Bosworth Field and the Wars of the Roses*, Macmillan, London, 1966.

Rowse, A. L., 'Alltyrynys and the Cecils', *English Historical Review*, Vol. 74, 1960.

Royal Commission on Ancient and Historical Monuments in Wales and Mon., *Carmarthenshire Inventory*, 1917. Tomb of Sir Rhys ap Thomas, s.n. St Peter's Church, Carmarthen.

Skeel, C. A. J., 'Wales Under Henry VII', in R. W. Seton-Watson (ed.), *Tudor Studies*, University of London Press, 1924.

Spurrell, G. W., *The History of Carew*, Spurrell, Carmarthen, 1922.

Vergil, Polydore, *Three Books of English History*, Sir H. Ellis (Ed.), Camden Society, Old Series, London, 1844.

Williams, Glanmor, *The Welsh Church from Conquest to Reformation*, University of Wales Press, Cardiff, 1976 ed.

Williams, Glanmor, 'Prophecy, Politics, and Poetry in Medieval Wales', in H. Hearder & H. R. Loyn (eds.), *British Government and Administration: Essays Presented to S. B. Chrimes*, University of Wales Press, Cardiff, 1974.

Williams, Glanmor, *Henry Tudor and Wales*, University of Wales Press, Cardiff, 1985.

Williams, Glanmor, *Recovery, Reorientation and Reformation: Wales c.1415-1642.* Vol. II, *The History of Wales.* Oxford University Press/University of Wales Press, 1987.

Williams, Gruffydd Aled, 'The Bardic Road to Bosworth: A Welsh View of Henry Tudor', in *Trans. Hon. Soc. of Cymmrodorion*, London, 1986.

Williams, Sir Ifor & Williams, John Ll. (Eds.), *Gwaith Guto'r Glyn*, University of Wales, Press, Cardiff, 1939.

Williams. Rhys Dafys, 'Forfeited Lands of Rhys ap Gruffydd', in *Carmarthen Antiquary*, Vol. V, 1964-69.

Williams, W. Llewelyn, 'A Welsh Insurrection', *Y Cymmrodor*, Vol. 16, 1903.

Williams-Jones, K., 'Another "Indenture of the Marches" 1 March 1490', in *Bulletin of the Board of Celtic Studies*, Vol. 24, 1970-72.

Wynn, Sir John, *The History of the Gwydir Family and Memoirs*, Edited with an Introduction by J. Gwynfor Jones, Gomer Press, Llandysul, 1991.

INDEX

Abermarlais, 5-6, 11-12, 14, 15, 64, 68-9

Beaufort, Lady Margaret, 7
Blackheath, battle of, 56
Boulogne, expedition against, 55
Bosworth Field, battle of, 45-7
Bray, Reginald, 34
Buckingham, Henry Stafford, 2nd Duke of, 27-9
Butler, Arnold, of Coedcanlas, 32, 38

Cae Gurwen, manor of, 14
Carew castle, 15, 59-61, 65
Carmarthen castle, 3, 5, 12, 24, 63
Carreg Cennen castle, 3, 10, 55
Crug, near Llandeilo, 1, 4
Cwrt Bryn-y-beirdd, 5

Dale, 33, 38
Dafydd Nanmor, 26
Dafydd Llwyd ap Llywelyn (of Mathafarn), 13-14, 21, 36, 41
Dinefwr (Dynevor): lordship or demesnes of, 4-5, 14, 83; castle, 4, 10, 55, 63
Dwnn, Lewis, 1, 2, 15

Geoffrey of Monmouth, 20-1
Gruffydd, Elis, 'the soldier of Calais', 17

Gruffydd ap Nicholas, 3-5, 8-9, 18, 25, 61, 62
Gruffydd ap Rhys (d.1521), 71, 72
Gower, lordship of, 14-15, 18, 64
Gorlech, Dafydd, 36
Guto'r Glyn, 15, 21, 22, 48, 67

Francis, Duke of Brittany, 30

Henry VII (Henry Tudor, Earl of Richmond): descent and childhood, 7-8, 26; in exile, 26-7; relations with French court, 30-1; lands at Dale, 38-9; victory at Bosworth Field, 45-7; establishment of reign, 51-4
Henry ap Gwilym, 15-16
Herbert, Sir William, Earl of Pembroke (d. 1469) 10, 15, 16, 21, 26-7, 61
Huw Cae Llwyd, 65

Ieuan Rudd, 65
Iorwerth Fynglwyd, 66, 76-7

Katherine of Valois, 7
Kidwelly: lordship of, 3; castle, 55, 63, 66

Landimore, manor of, 14
Lewis Glyn Cothi, 4, 8-9, 11, 13, 16, 21, 36-7, 53, 55, 67-9